Praise for *Footmark*

'Lucid, poetic and fascinating – a beautiful journey through time and across diverse landscapes. From ancient hominin footprints to holloways, from cattle drovers to pilgrims, Leary explores how journeys make us human.'

ALICE ROBERTS, anatomist, author and broadcaster

'Engaging, authoritative and full of fascinating stories of the past. This book shows that life is not centred on hearth and house, as we are so often told, but is shaped by relentless movement, along tracks and trails. By focusing on mobility, Jim Leary has managed to reanimate the past, revealing the hidden but vital contribution that migration has always made to the shaping of the world.'

RAY MEARS, bushcraft expert, author and broadcaster

'A gentle, personal and very readable book that gives life to the dynamic sequence of activity, effort and extraordinary determination that makes up our human past.'

JULIA BLACKBURN, author of *Time Song*

'I loved this book. It's a highly readable account of how and why people have moved around on the surface of the earth, across land and sea. It ranges from prehistoric footpaths to Roman and medieval roads and includes fascinating pieces on ancient ships and boats. What makes this book so special is that everything is discussed within the context of life at the time: who were using the paths or the boats and why were they doing it?'

FRANCIS PRYOR, archaeologist and author

'*Footmarks* takes us on a magnificent voyage tracing the fascinating history and restless patterns of human movement. From ancient children playing and scrambling, through all manner of ambling, trudging, sprinting and roaming, Leary explores the many ways archaeology can reveal the dynamism of past lives and the way in which we both make and are made by the paths we take. Brimming with detail yet written lightly and with unashamed affection, this delightful book shows how we are all part of a vast, whirling dance that's been going on for millennia.'

REBECCA WRAGG SYKES, author of *Kindred*

'Archaeological writing at its best: lucid, rational and deeply woven with the real lives of real people from the past. You'll never think about – or walk around – historic sites the same way again.'

MARY-ANN OCHOTA, broadcaster and anthropologist

'*Footmarks* is a joy. A dance with our predecessors, through settings that feel by turns intimate and familiar, then questing and bold. By animating the ancient past Leary reminds us that far from being distant observers of the ancient past, we are a product of it, in both spirit and substance.'

AMY-JANE BEER, naturalist and author of *The Flow*

'Jim Leary takes us into the little-explored realm of ancient movement. We walk with hominins and Neanderthals, explore deep caves, herd cattle, and become pilgrims, ocean voyagers and long-distance walkers ... This beautifully written, entertaining essay melds personal experience with archaeological and historical wisdom. The result is a truly remarkable and original book that thinks profoundly about the past. Read this and be inspired!'

BRIAN FAGAN, Emeritus Professor of Anthropology, University of California and author

'With charm, wit and warmth, we are led through an alternative archaeology, one where movement and mobility take precedence over settlement and sedentism ... *Footmarks* reminds us that the restless journey and some of the most meaningful experiences along its path leave no trace but the imprints where feet have trodden.'

ALEX LANGLANDS, author of *Craeft*

'Engaging and impassioned, *Footmarks* is an enchanting stroll through the deep history of human wanderings across the world. This book will delight and entice all who muse on the ways in which we have ever walked upon this earth. A triumph!'

JAMES CANTON, author of *The Oak Papers*

'Archaeologists have a superpower: time travel. Their digs show us cold hearths and colder graves, but as Jim Leary shows in this gripping read, the past was hot-blooded and alive with the movement of people who loved and laughed as we do.'

JOHN HARRISON, award-winning travel writer

'Jim Leary's archaeological passion is "paths over pyramids" and *Footmarks* is as lively and entertaining an exploration of human wanderings as you could ever hope to read. It links our colourful and complex history to how we live today, clearing up a few notable misconceptions along the way. This compelling, highly original book will change the way you think about landscape and our place within it.'

IAN CARTER, author of *Human, Nature.*

'A touching, illuminating and fascinating book. Leary is a great guide through our restless history.'

ROB COWEN, author *Common Ground*

Footmarks

Footmarks

A Journey Into our Restless Past

Jim Leary

ICON

This edition published in the UK and USA in 2024 by
Icon Books Ltd, Omnibus Business Centre,
39–41 North Road, London N7 9DP
email: info@iconbooks.com
www.iconbooks.com

ISBN: 978-183773-025-4
ebook: 978-183773-026-1

Typeset by SJmagic DESIGN SERVICES, India

Printed and bound in Great Britain

CONTENTS

ABOUT THE AUTHOR

Dr Jim Leary is an archaeologist and Senior Lecturer at the University of York, and a Fellow of the Society of Antiquaries. He has directed major excavations across Britain, including Silbury Hill in Wiltshire, the largest Neolithic monument in Europe. A passionate walker, much of his research is centred on the way people moved around in the past.

DEDICATION

For mum, dad, Piers, and Justin

TIMELINE

Before Present
Palaeolithic ('Old Stone Age': from around 1 million to 12,000 years ago in Britain)

3.66 million	Laetoli footprints made
1.52 million	Koobi Fora footprints made
950,000–850,000	Happisburgh footprints made
135,000	Theopetra Cave footprints made
130,000–100,000	Neanderthals already travelling to Crete by sea
80,000	Le Rozel footprints made
50,000	Humans already travelling to Australia by sea
25,000–20,000	Willandra Lakes footprints made
17,200–16,500	Tuc d'Audoubert Cave used by humans
14,000	Bàsura Cave footprints made

Before Common Era (BCE)
Mesolithic ('Middle Stone Age': hunter-gatherers, from around 10,000 BCE to 4000 BCE in Britain)

9300–8500	Star Carr Mesolithic site in use
7000–4000	Formby Point footprints made
5700–4000	Skateholm Mesolithic cemetery in use
5500–5000	Severn Estuary footprints made

Neolithic ('New Stone Age': first farmers, from around 4000 BCE to 2500 BCE in Britain)

3807/6	Sweet Track constructed
c. 3500	Horse first domesticated in Kazakhstan (although not regularly used as mount until 2200 BCE)
c. 3500	Wheel in use in parts of continental Europe from this time
3500–3000	Cursus monuments constructed in Britain
3230	'Ötzi' the Iceman dies
2500–2000	Major monument construction across Britain: Silbury Hill, Marden henge, The Sanctuary, Woodhenge, Avebury, etc.

Bronze Age (2500 BCE to 800 BCE in Britain)

2380–2290	Amesbury Archer dies
2049	Seahenge constructed
c. 1800	Ferriby boats in East Yorkshire constructed
1750–1550	Nebra sky disc in use
1740–210	Uffington White Horse created
1575–1520	Dover Bronze Age boat, Europe's oldest sea-going vessel, constructed
1400–1300	Trundholm sun chariot in use
1370	Egtved Girl dies
c. 1300	Skrydstrup Woman dies
c. 1300	Wheel introduced to Britain around this time
c. 1100–800	Must Farm settlement in use

Iron Age (800 BCE to 43 CE in Britain)

c. 600	Roos Carr figurines created
405–380	Tollund Man dies
400–200	Grauballe Man dies
350–150	Pocklington chariot burial
200–5	Sharpstone Hill Iron Age road constructed
2 BCE–119 CE	Lindow Man dies

Common Era (CE)
Medieval (450 to 1500)

500–700	Sutton Hoo cemeteries in use
750–1066	Viking activity taking place around Britain
1061	Our Lady of Walsingham shrine constructed
1066	Battle of Stamford Bridge (and the Norman Conquest)
c. 1200s	Chartres Cathedral labyrinth constructed
1285	The Statute of Winchester
1388	The Statute of Cambridge
c. 1400	Chaucer's *Canterbury Tales* completed by this time
1414	The Pleasance at Kenilworth constructed
1450–1700	The process of early Enclosure takes place
1500	Wharram Percy largely abandoned

Post-medieval (1500 onwards)

1530	Henry VIII passes the Egyptians Act
1549	Kett's Rebellion takes place

PART 1

Close to home

1. THE STILLNESS OF THE PAST

*In which a personal tragedy leads to another way
of thinking about the past*

Imagine the world we live in without movement. As if
we all instantly froze, to be discovered centuries later,
just as we are. What significance would archaeologists of
the future find in the places we inhabit, or the routes that
we travel? What would those archaeologists think about
the place where you just happen to be right now?

Places lose so much of their meaning when you take
out the movement. For too long, archaeology has sought
to understand the past by focusing on things that lie still.
How could it do otherwise? But life isn't still. It's full of
movement. Stillness is death.

*

3

At 6.30 in the morning, on the 12th of November in 2003, my elder brother was commuting on a busy country road. Recently married, and having moved house and jobs, he was full of optimism for his new life in the Lake District. A rustle in the bushes caused Piers to jump a little. A streak like a flash of fire – a fox perhaps? A jerk of the steering wheel caused his car to swerve. The swerve became a skid, a sliding motion across the lane, out of his allotted space of movement into oncoming traffic. A crashing, crushing, grinding. The coming together of flesh and glass and metal, and a life stopped.

Piers was nineteen months older than me. Sometimes his death feels as raw and fresh as if it were days ago, not years. But life has moved on – mine, my family's, his wife's. I have photographs of him to keep his memory close, and look at them often, although only three are out on display in my house, the others tucked away in a box under the stairs. One of these is from when we were young, perhaps five and six, standing in our garden with our younger brother Justin, the three of us carefree in our pyjamas. Another is from his wedding day, grinning awkwardly in his suit and cravat with one arm around our mother. The third is a small, standard-sized photograph in a glass clip frame. It sits on a windowsill in the living room, propped against a ceramic bowl. The image has faded in the sun and at some point, like my memories, it will disappear altogether.

This last image of him was snapped by a colleague at his leaving party just two or three days before his move north and the fateful commute. Piers stares down the camera, his collar up, index fingers out and thumbs up as if about to say 'Ayyy!', in the style of Fonzie from the

American sitcom *Happy Days*. A split second captured on film; a fleeting moment in time, long gone, showing his humour and joy. He was at the party to say goodbye to his friends, as he stood on the threshold between two jobs, between one place and another, and – although he didn't know it – between life and death.

My children only know him through these photos, as a series of static images in which he remains forever 29, and newly wed. Those of us who knew him remember that he was warm and funny and full of laughter and life. We remember his jokes, the easy way he made friends, and his distinctive swaying side-to-side walk that gave him a permanent jaunty look. But with the passing of time, he seems to have become frozen in the stillness of the past.

This is true of all history. Once, it was warm and full of life. Or cold, dark and miserable. But never motionless. My brother's death changed how I think about the past. I want to keep it alive. I do not want Piers, or any other part of history, to become inert. I want to reanimate it – all of it!

In this book, I will do that by exploring how people have moved, over millions of years.

*

Here is a different story.

On a warm summer's day, four young adults set off along the edge of an estuary. They walk alongside one another heading south-east. With every step their bare feet sink into the soft estuarine mud, which squeezes up through their toes and clamps around their heels. It sucks and squelches as they move. In the background are the cries of estuary birds and the sound of the gently ebbing tide, rippled by a briny breeze. Cutting through this is the excited chatter of children and the distant calls of their parents.

Perhaps they are on their way to collect something, or going home after delivering it. Or maybe they are out to do something entirely different. It could be that they are there for no particular reason at all, just out for a walk, to feel the summer sun on their necks and the cool, wet mud around their feet.

They stride at a brisk pace. At one stage, one of them sees something and veers left, crossing the paths of the others and causing them to bunch together momentarily before spreading out once more.

Nearby, a child of three or four plays with someone a few years older; perhaps a sibling. The younger of the two playfully, absent-mindedly, dances around the other, leaving an erratic array of footprints in the mud. Footmarks. The older one picks up something heavy – could it be the youngster? – and feels his or her feet sink, leaving noticeably deeper traces in the ground.

Elsewhere, a person steps out across the estuary in a straight line heading west. Certainty and purpose. This other person walks at a steady pace, despite sliding twice in the mud, and halts momentarily, feet side-by-side, before continuing.

Actions like these are the stuff of life. They could be from anytime and anywhere – today, yesterday, last century. These happened at the end of the sixth and beginning of the fifth millennium BCE,* towards the end of a period

---

* Before the Common Era. I will use BCE and CE – Common Era – throughout, instead of the rather old-fashioned BC/AD.

known as the Mesolithic; a time before farming and domesticated species, when people were hunters and gatherers. They happened at a place now known as Goldcliff; a series of glutinous and glistening mudflats on the coastal fringe of the Severn Estuary, south-east of the Welsh city of Newport. Few but fishermen, lugworm gatherers, and the odd team of archaeologists visit this barren landscape now, but it was once home to generations of families.

The evidence comes from footprint tracks exposed in banded sediments on the edge of a former river channel. The fine-grained silt within which the clearest footprints were found would have been laid down during spring and summer months. In some, you can see cracks in the mud suggesting that it was hot when the footprint was made. The prints were sealed by coarser-grained sandy deposits during the following autumn and winter, preserving them for future archaeologists to find and excavate.

These fragmented, fossilised tracks indicate the trails of humans and animals. From them we can record the length of their stride, as well as the pace at which each person was walking. The faster they ran, the further apart we find their footprints. A slow and steady speed leaves regular footprints, close together. From the size of their feet, we can say a certain amount about their age and body size.

More than anything, they provide tangible evidence for the currents of life that make up actual human existence. These people lived and loved and died in the world we now occupy, and came to know their physical world *by the way they moved through it*.

Their footprints confirm the eternal human compulsion to roam. But what they don't make entirely clear is also fascinating. Were these people engaged in the kind of everyday pottering that we forget as soon as it's finished, or some purposeful life journey of the kind they might have talked about for years? To an archaeologist, both kinds of movement are crucial to a better understanding of the past.

Archaeology has tended to show us cold hearths and colder graves, but the past was hot-blooded and alive with activity. When we incorporate our own restless ways into how we see the past, everything changes. Ideas about our origins, and about ourselves today, become much more exciting.

Without journeying, humankind would have struggled a brief while in Africa, then vanished. Our ability to walk over long distances, driven by our innate curiosity, explains how we have occupied almost every corner of the planet. Moving makes us everything that we are and ever have been.

*

Mathematicians often talk about feeling as if they exist in two parallel worlds: one their real life, the other an underlying mathematical world ordering and connecting everything together. I feel the same about archaeology. I have my normal, daily life in which I operate, but all around me is another, more shadowy one. A sensory, synaesthetic world, made up of echoes from the past. I take note of lumps, dips and ridges in fields, and lines of hedgerows, or an out-of-place building and an unusually shaped street. And, whether I want to or not, my brain clicks and whirrs and tries to make sense of it all; tries to order it, and understand how it came to be. As I walk down a path, I note the features and plants alongside it, how deep the path has been eroded, whether it is lined with earthen banks, drystone walls or a hedgerow, and if so whether that hedge is mature or grown-out, predominantly hawthorn or made up of other species. As we'll see later, these tiny details can be telling. While I walk through a landscape I mentally reconstruct, as best I can, its history and try to feel the feet of the past.

I suspect all archaeologists are like this.

I don't know at what point I became interested in archaeology, but I know Piers was involved in the process. Long before me, he had wanted to study archaeology at university. As it happens, he went down more of a historian's path. But I think our interest started much earlier. We lived in Cyprus when we were young. Our house was surrounded by Mediterranean scrubland that was scattered throughout with pieces of Roman and Ancient Greek pottery, like olives in a salad. On one occasion, snorkelling in the sea near home, Piers pulled out a chunk of amphora he'd spotted washed into the shallows. Terracotta in colour, it consisted of just the neck and handle, and was about a foot long. But for the chalky encrustations of the sea, it would have been smooth to the touch. What struck me at the time, treading water and turning it around in my pruned and salty hands, was not its age, or shape, or what it might say about trade, but something else altogether. A thumbprint, presumably the maker's, had been impressed and then fired into the top of the handle. This print spoke to me of the physicality of the making process, the feel and smell of the soft, pliable clay, the humanness of it all. History, Ancient

History, and Classics could intimidate me with their vast scale, but here I felt a personal connection to another human – someone, as I imagined it, just like me.

After Piers died, I took the amphora fragment. I still have it, and I still have that sense of connection to the past. That connection has a name: it is called archaeology.

*

Walk past a construction site today and you may well see teams of archaeologists uncovering the pits and postholes of past lives before the new building – homes, offices, or whatever it is to be – destroys them. This world of development-led archaeology is how I took my first steps in the profession, in the 1990s, after I finished my degree. On those digs, we were like Forrest Gump dipping randomly into his box of chocolates: we never knew what we were getting next. Would it be deep medieval or Roman deposits within the city walls? A sequence of Saxon houses in Covent Garden? Or nothing at all, just modern rubble on top of natural ground? I loved it! Friendships flourish with uncertainty and in difficult situations, and love can blossom over shared conversations and a packed lunch. I met my future wife in a muddy archaeologists' Portakabin.

We excavated within the basements of buildings, the process of demolition going on around us, but more often we dug in the open air, either surrounded by the ruins of the earlier building, or on a brown, rubble-strewn site surrounded by wooden hoarding. (Just occasionally – rarely, but it did happen from time to time – we found ourselves on a pleasant greenfield site.) Working alongside us we often had a crew of, by then, quite elderly Irish men. They would be there to dig holes for services for the new buildings, but they also looked after our ever-deepening trenches, ensuring they were safe, and shored when necessary. They might also monitor and maintain our growing spoil heaps. Frequently these men were our lifeline. Friendly, charming and endlessly entertaining, these old boys, who stood out on site in their wrinkled and dusty linen jackets, were expert diggers, genuine craftsmen of the shovel. A skill learnt over decades of physical work. They also knew the value of a good cup of tea, and a cracking joke. The machine drivers were important too. A good driver could make a site. The best of them, at the time, revered by all who met him, was a man known as Grease Gun Jimmy, named because of his propensity to extrude grease into the arm of his digger every few minutes to create smoother movements. Watching him at work was like watching an expert ballet dancer; man and machine as one, the mechanical arm and bucket an extension of his own arm and hand. Many of these men had moved to London from Ireland in the 1960s and 1970s to work in construction. Migrants in search of work, adventure, and a different life. Few are left now: a lot of them returned to Ireland during the financial crisis of the noughties, and I daresay – although it pains me to think so – many are probably no longer with us.

I was always struck by how all this action and noise above ground – the movement of hand- and machine-dug earth and endless flows of people – contrasted with the static and silent understanding we imposed on the lives we were excavating below ground.

Years later I excavated some magnificent ancient monuments working for what was then called English

Heritage (later it became Historic England). Marden henge in the Vale of Pewsey in Wiltshire was one of them. We will hear more about this huge Neolithic monument later in the book, but in 2010 and 2015, excavating inside it, we uncovered the well-preserved chalk floor of a 4,500-year-old building. A large hearth dominated the centre, and around the fire, scattered over the floor, were pieces of pottery and flint flakes, lying exactly where they were originally dropped. Outside the building was a pile of pig bones, representing joints of meat roasted on the bone. Mixed in with them were pieces of a type of Neolithic pottery known as Grooved Ware, so called due to the incised geometric grooves that decorate it. The larger Grooved Ware pots are big and flat-bottomed, resembling a bucket, and were likely used for cooking, particularly pork; the smaller ones probably held food and drink, including milk, but perhaps also beer. This pile was not a rubbish dump that had accumulated over time, but the result of a single action; the remains of a feast. Covered over with a Neolithic bank of earth, it had been preserved for us to find thousands of years later. This scene was an astounding discovery – once in a lifetime – but what really struck me was how much it looked like the morning after the night before; the music stopped, debris strewn around, and all partygoers gone. In the Neolithic, this feast would have been accompanied by music, dancing and whirling; storytelling, chanting and chatter. I'm saying that like I know – of course I don't, but it's not unreasonable to think so, considering what we know of human nature. We routinely don't think about such things. It would have been heady and sensuous with the smell of wood smoke, roast pork and beer, combined with flickering flames, garish costumes and, well, who knows but perhaps the consumption of hallucinogenic mushrooms.

But archaeologists always miss the party.

And this stillness we uncover feeds into how society generally learns about the past. Newspaper headlines, when a well-preserved archaeological site is discovered, describe it as 'frozen in time'. 'Britain's Pompeii' is another favourite. The implication is that something cataclysmic happened, rendering the site motionless. People stilled, like statues, with their arms raised up in horror. With the advent of movies about the past, this mindset has started to change. Thanks to films like *Jurassic Park*, for example, it's easy for people today to imagine the movement of dinosaurs, whether or not the film is really accurate. But archaeology is still too often presented as a still photograph. The significance of movement is overlooked.

The enormous Neolithic mound of Silbury Hill in Wiltshire is another wonderful English Heritage monument I worked on. For over a year in 2007 and 2008, I led a team of archaeologists to excavate a tunnel into the centre of it to allow engineers to stabilise a collapse that could be seen on the summit. We also hoped to understand something of how it was made, and glimpse at possible reasons why. One of the most striking things we discovered during our time in this tunnel was how, from the moment the mound was created until at least the medieval period, and probably much later, it was in constant motion, being added to and dug into, changed and altered. Quite a contrast with the way it was being managed, and still is now; covered in short-cropped grass, like a suburban garden or a golf course, all traces of humanity removed, as if preserved in aspic or covered by a bell jar. A precious artefact in need of protection from a dangerous world. Quite right too, you might say, but it does have the effect of imposing stillness that wasn't there before. It reminds me of the way oral stories are passed down generationally from parent to child: living things that alter as times change but which, once they are written down, become static and not to be messed with. And that can be deadening.[1]

*

When I mention to other archaeologists that I'm writing about movement in the past, they occasionally reply: 'Of course people moved around. We know that! It's obvious.'

Well, sometimes the obvious needs stating, so that its significance can be seen afresh. And sometimes the obvious is all we have. We rely on it to create our best guess about how people lived in the deepest past. When somebody makes a discovery, we can set aside our guessing (if it's been proved to be mistaken) or build on it (if it is validated). One way to make those guesses is to think about the ways we move ourselves, in the present and in recent history. We can ask ourselves if those movements are culturally specific or intrinsically human – and if they're intrinsically human we can assume that our prehistoric ancestors moved that way too.

For too long, there has been a tendency to focus on the fixed and more tangible elements of the past, on 'places' rather than the movement to, from, and around them.

On the one hand, this is understandable because with 'place' there is something to see and excavate. We can be 'in' a settlement, and 'go' to a monument. Archaeologists like neatly bounded sites that we can draw around and, if the sites are nationally important, secure with legal protection as Scheduled Monuments. We like to impose boundaries, turning sites into containers of, and for, archaeology.[2]

But by studying *only* the site we unthinkingly impose stillness on the past – a form of disenchantment that can rob it of all wonder.

I can get so frustrated when I read articles and books about the movement of people or objects that mention only the place they came from or went to, and nothing about the meaningful movements in between.

It is the movements in between that are the important elements of life. 'Life unfolds,' says the anthropologist and thinker Tim Ingold, echoing the writer and journey-man Bruce Chatwin, 'not in places, but along paths.' We miss the action, the real life, if we don't look at people's movements.[3]

Of course, places are important. But we can afford to recognise that they are made by the restless patterns of people moving between them and through them: from one chamber to another, in and out of shops and houses, through tangles of alleys, plazas, streets, and roads. Places are designed for access and movement, and as we see in our own times they pulsate with life.[4]

Movement defies the notion of a neatly bounded site or monument. Of all sites, routeways are especially hard for heritage managers to protect, since they are long and linear, and run across land owned by multiple people. They are also seen as the opposite of monuments because they are often created by being worn down as opposed to built up; a negative feature, rather than a positive. Yet they are every bit as monumental. More so, in fact: they don't represent the actions of a few builders over a defined period, but the feet of many over vast lengths of time, as we'll see in a later chapter. Out of the 20,000 Scheduled Monuments in England, the only protected holloways – deeply incised paths, also known as sunken ways – that I can find are short sections that have been included, almost incidentally, as components of other monuments. Few, if any, are scheduled on their own, due to their intrinsic importance. They are not automatically afforded the protection the more obvious archaeological sites receive. And who knows how many holloways there actually are; I doubt anyone has ever attempted an audit of them the way they have other monuments. But that has to be a starting point for protection.

In the village I live in, the earthwork remains of a medieval motte and bailey castle is a Scheduled Monument, but the tangled and radiating holloways – earthworks every bit as impressive as the motte and of the same date, or earlier – are not. So, the landowners are free to scour them away, which they have done. Or, in the case of one I recently walked along, dug into it and lined the bottom with hardcore. At least it's preserved now, you might say, but like writing down an oral story or pinning a butterfly, it's no longer alive. That seems to me a very great shame. And that's just one small, personal example. Extend that out across the British Isles, and across Europe and beyond, and you start to see the extent of the problem. That's just one reason why we need to talk about movement in archaeology.

Moving is so natural, so everyday, that it's easy to overlook, but we miss the real action when we do that. By following footsteps, we find the texture of paths and the places they connect. We hear settlements alive and full of busy people; the hubbub of business, the shouts of street vendors, the din from the inns. We see gossip spreading along lanes and alleys – *these* were the conduits where real life happened. Rhythms of all kinds pulsed through places and paths. Just think of the vibrant routeways that led to and from the Athenian Agora, medieval castles and royal palaces. Or the parks where nineteenth-century bourgeois Parisians would promenade along manicured avenues. Or the roads on which people routinely commute.

By shifting our focus to the way people moved, we infuse the past again with the dynamism and vital force it once contained, letting it live in the present. You can try this for yourself: next time you are in a museum, looking at motionless artefacts, take a second to imagine what they tell you about human mobility. It will change your perspective. This is the task I have set myself with this book: to think again about the stilled objects, monuments and paths around us, and to reanimate them.

I want to dig up the extraordinary stories of people on the move, not only because I like to share those stories but because new developments in archaeology are changing fundamental ideas about how our forebears lived. Archaeologists, osteologists, isotope specialists and geneticists are throwing into the air many settled ideas, such as: Were hunter-gatherers really more mobile than farmers? Have women travellers always been more constrained than men? Were the big innovations of farming and metalworking introduced by immigrants? And did prehistoric societies have their own charismatic adventurer-leaders – their own Shackletons and Edmund Hillarys?

*

The process of walking rarely follows a straight line with a beginning, middle and end. It is spidery and complex, with frequent diversions around things, forking and then reconnecting paths, and inevitably some retracing of steps. Only by looking back do you see that you have been pathmaking. This book takes a similarly loose approach. We will travel millions of years through the Palaeolithic, Mesolithic, Neolithic, Bronze and Iron Ages, and across the periods of written history, encountering cultures and people such as the Beakers, the Vikings and the French Impressionists. We'll tramp through mud, take bicycles, horses and boats. Most of the time, we'll stay in and around the UK – under burial mounds, circling henges, trespassing on private land, getting wet feet on beaches, tramping through the woodlands of Oxfordshire and digging beneath the streets of the City of London. But occasionally we will find ourselves further afield: in Africa, Denmark, the Alps, the Russian Steppes, Turkey.

Using the very latest science and technology, we'll analyse chemical isotopes in the teeth and bones of the long-dead, count tree-rings, and map the ancient DNA of entire populations.

Walking alongside us will be a remarkable crowd of archaeologists, anthropologists, writers, sociologists, and even the odd movie star. With their help, I hope to share with you my own excitement as we find answers to things that were, until very recently, mysteries.

As you read, you may expect to follow a particular line, only to realise that we have taken a detour. I hope you will enjoy this approach and will take from it what most pleases you – just as I imagine those wanderers on the Severn Estuary, 7,000 years ago, might have stopped on their way to pick up anything that caught their eye.

In other words, welcome to the new 'mobile archaeology': the archaeology of movement, shining its wobbly torchlight against our previously murky understanding.

Humans have always been on the move; it defines our nature, from the moment we are born – in fact, even before that. So we will begin our journey with the human body. We will look at how walking is sensual and experiential, before moving on to how we turn it into something fashion-conscious and culturally specific: a performance.

We will see that mobility has different meanings according to the individual, the time, and the culture: it can be freedom, opportunity, progress, or constraint and rebellion. It has been historicised, romanticised, but also feared and controlled.

Our journey will take in footprint trails left a million years ago along the north Norfolk coast in the UK, and early hunter-gatherer footprints from a cave in France. We will see how these trails become tracks, paths, and eventually roads; from prehistoric wooden trackways to ridgeways, holloways, droveways, green ways, corpse roads, and Roman roads. Each of these physical features has a story to tell us. These are the historical counterparts of the modern roads on which people drive daily.

We'll see that the way people walk, and the pathmaking they leave behind, depends on *why* they're moving: a hunter's progress is different from a shepherd's, which is different again from a cattle herder's. Each one – walking alone, in company, with dogs or with livestock – perceives the landscape around them slightly differently.

By looking through a wayfarer's eyes we'll discover how people on the move engaged with our three-dimensional, lumpy, bumpy, weather-beaten world, and we'll see that the landscape has been folded and moulded to our travelling needs.

Having started with individuals' footsteps, we'll progress steadily through longer trips, and the final chapters will take us on the giant human journeys that people have made across continents and oceans. We will assess the pathways of migration, in wave after wave, through every part of the globe, and ask what it tells us about the transmission of individuals, populations, and entirely new ways of life.

The past is made up of travelling, wandering, tracking, herding, riding, sailing and migration. Archaeology is increasingly coming to recognise this restlessness. I hope that by bringing this into view, the past – and with it my brother – will never be still.

2. MOVING MATTERS

....

*In which we see that movement forms the foundation of our
thoughts, our skeleton, and life itself*

....

Without movement, life is not possible. To be alive is
to move. It is primal.

'Seeing comes before words,' says John Berger in his
classic book *Ways of Seeing*. 'The child looks and rec-
ognizes before it can speak.' But movement comes even
before seeing: a child moves before it looks, while still in
the womb.

We discover ourselves through movement, and we
make sense of the world, and all the things in it, by
moving, by reaching, grabbing and grasping. It forms
our basic perceptual system and structures our knowledge. As we journey through life, we continue to make
sense of the world, to know it, by exploring it through
movement.[1]

It happens spontaneously; we don't have to think
about it because movement *is* thought.

The linguist George Lakoff and philosopher Mark
Johnson have highlighted how embedded movement
is within our thoughts. A line of thought is a path along
which our opinions travel. They proceed 'step by step',

'arriving' at the next point and hoping to 'reach' a conclusion. At times our mind 'races' along. At others it gets 'stuck'. Occasionally our mind 'wanders', or goes off on 'flights' of fancy. We 'put' an idea into people's heads, and hope it doesn't 'go over' them, or be 'beyond their grasp'. With a good argument you can 'wrong-foot' someone and put them on the 'back foot'. But 'best foot' forward. If you have 'one foot in the grave' you are likely to be on your 'last legs'.

In many societies, time is conceptualised as moving. The future is often understood to be in front of us, the past behind. We face forward, towards the future. We look 'forward' to things. Time is 'coming' or long since 'gone'. It 'flies' if you're having fun, but we don't want it to 'pass us by'. Sometimes time is stationary, and it is we who do the moving – we 'approach' the end of the year, for example, or move 'through the years'.[2]

Movement pervades our entire conceptual system, leaving a long trail of metaphorical language. It is used to grasp abstract concepts such as time. And perhaps that's not surprising, because the act of walking keeps our brain moving.

Long periods of immobility weaken our muscles, alter blood pressure and metabolic rate, put pressure on our lower backs, and, as we'll see in a moment, actually change our skeleton. Stillness causes our brain to slow down, reducing alertness. Walking improves all these problems. It opens our lungs, and allows us to see, hear, smell, and connect with the world and the beings within it.[3] Walking has helped me overcome some difficult times.

Walking makes us feel good, and think better thoughts: our mind wandering as our feet do. Some of the greatest thinkers were passionate walkers, going back at least as far as the Peripatetics of Ancient Greece. The Greek sage walking along a colonnade followed by his pupils may be a bit of a caricature, but the historian Diogenes Laërtius suggests that Plato walked and taught at the same time. And Plato's protégé, Aristotle, was known as 'Walker', perhaps due to teaching on the hoof.[4]

I love to teach my students like this now, in the open air rather than a stuffy lecture theatre. That's what a field-trip is – mobile teaching.

The philosopher and political thinker Jean-Jacques Rousseau declared that he could only think when walking. He describes his walks in *Reveries of a Solitary Walker*, and the 'flights of thought' that were sparked by them. Immanuel Kant took walks around his home town with such regularity that he was known as the 'Königsberg clock'. His route through the park was later named 'the philosopher's walk'. Friedrich Nietzsche actually believed that walking produced qualitatively better ideas: 'Only ideas *won by walking* have any value,' he asserted in *Twilight of the Idols*.

Bruce Chatwin was a nomadic writer, and former archaeology student, who believed that the world reveals itself to those on foot: 'Man's real home is not a house, but the Road, and life itself is a journey to be walked on foot,' he wrote. 'The act of journeying contributes towards a sense of physical and mental well-being.' Similar ideas are highlighted in the diaries of the ecologist and activist Roger Deakin ('It's when I do all my thinking – when I'm walking'), and in the work of many other wonderful writers, such as Rebecca Solnit, Robert Macfarlane and Geoff Nicholson.[5]

Artists too have used walking as a creative practice. One, Richard Long, went on to make walking into a performance piece: *A Line Made by Walking* (1967) consists of a photograph of a path he made through a grass field. A slightly later work is *A Line the Length of a Straight Walk from the Bottom to the Top of Silbury Hill* (1970), a spiral of muddy footprints representing the route the title describes. I know the route well, having walked it many times when I worked on, and inside, that massive Neolithic monument.

And the artist Antony Gormley buried a life-sized statue upside down outside the McDonald Institute for Archaeological Research at the University of Cambridge, with only its soles showing. To see it was like finding the reverse of the footprint tracks described earlier. Gormley's artwork is called 'Earthbound Plant', and it gives a strange prickly feeling to stand directly on the statue's soles knowing that a full-length body lies directly below, like some sort of solid bronze reflection. Each time I've done this, I have an eerie feeling that when I walk away the statue walks with me, following me in its upside-down world. Perhaps it is still with me.

*

We don't just think in movement; we *are* movements. Kinaesthesia, deriving from the Greek words *kinein* (to move) and *aesthesia* (sensation), is the awareness of the position and movement of your body. It is our non-verbal movement sense. Dancers must hone it assiduously.

And not only dancers. Moving in the world, we are in constant contact with its contours and shape. It can feel as if there is no separation between us and the world. We experience the world, and the things in it, through bodily actions, feeling what it is like to move from one place to another, or pick up an object and cause it to shift. We learn the meaning of things and understand their qualities through kinaesthesia.

Regular movements change and shape our bodies. Far from being a fixed structure, the skeleton is plastic and mouldable, imperfect and breakable, vulnerable to disease and decay, and mobility scores itself into the body. Different habitual actions, over a person's lifetime, put strain on the skeleton. As a result, new bone tissue is preferentially added to the shafts of the bones under strain, changing their shape so that they can withstand the load. People who regularly walk or run have thicker lower limb bones, while those who use their arms a lot will have more robust upper limbs.

We can see this in modern sportspeople. Studies have shown that swimmers and cricketers have pronounced bone growth in their arms, while cross-country runners and hockey players have the same in their legs. If someone uses one side of their body more than the other, this will lead to asymmetric bone growth: tennis players have considerably thicker bones on their playing side than their non-playing side.

It works both ways, so that decreased activity leads to bone loss, and more delicate bones.

What this means for the archaeologist is that the body can provide insights into the repetitive movements of people who lived in the distant past. The study of human remains allows us to reconstruct, to a certain degree, different activities across that person's lifetime. As with modern tennis players, the arms of archers are often detectable from skeletal remains, but not in the way you might think since they tend to show greater symmetry. Some skeletons recovered from the wreck of the *Mary Rose*, Henry VIII's flagship that sank in the Solent just off the south coast of England in 1545, show evidence for marked symmetry in their arm bones. This indicates that they likely pulled powerful longbows, which required immense strength from their non-dominant 'bow' arm compared to their 'draw' arm, evening out any natural difference between them. These same skeletons also exhibit repetitive stress injuries and abnormalities in their shoulders and lower spine, consistent with these actions.

By looking at large groups of human remains, we can see broader changes in cultural and behavioural patterns across different time periods, or even diversities within communities, such as between men and women. We can see high levels of walking among early human groups – Neanderthals, for example – as well as repetitive scraping tasks. A few years ago, I excavated the skeleton of a Bronze Age teenage boy from a site in Wiltshire, not far from Marden henge, that showed signs that his young and still developing body had been put under quite considerable physical stress. His thighs had extra muscle attachments for his glutes, suggesting that his legs were muscular and sportsman-like. But there was damage to his knees, likely the result of frequently walking uphill. His shoulders similarly had large muscle attachments, and lesions on his elbows indicated that his arms were undertaking strenuous activity. All this would have been the result of travel and toil; the daily drudge of hefting and heaving, cutting and constructing that no doubt kept the wheels of his way of life turning.

By studying the skeletal evidence in archaeology, we can infer many changes to subsistence activities, such as hunting or foraging over wide ranges, actions associated with herding animals, or the impact of agriculture. We can see how the physical terrain influences the size and shape of bones, like my teenage boy, so that walking in rugged and mountainous environments will lead to robust bones.[6]

It is partly because our skeleton is so adaptable that humans have been able to colonise different environments around the world. Our movements – and the landscapes where they take place – are literally written into our bones, ingrained in the skeleton.

And recent developments have allowed us to know more about the movement of individuals by studying their remains. For a long time, archaeology was regarded as strictly one of the humanities, but today archaeologists specialise in a variety of scientific disciplines and are as likely to wear a lab coat as we are to go out into the field. Among the new techniques developed to understand the past, the study of stable isotopes still blows my mind, because it tells us a great deal about how individuals moved around.

The water we drink contains trace elements of the bedrock it percolates through. Plants similarly absorb chemicals from the geology they grow on. As our teeth form, they absorb the chemical signatures from water and food, and it becomes fixed in our tooth enamel. Bones absorb these isotopes too. In this way, we take on the elements – the isotopes – of the particular geological region we grew up in as our teeth and bones were growing and developing.

This means that we can analyse teeth and bones to identify the general geological region a person spent their childhood, and compare it to where they were buried. In this way, we can see something of that person's movement over a lifetime. And because bone and teeth develop at different times within our lives, we might be able to see changes in locations at other stages of their life, depending on what teeth or part of the skeleton we analyse. Enamel from a person's first molar forms before birth, and continues forming until around the third birthday, providing information about the place of their childhood origin. Permanent teeth will have formed by the time they reach nine years, while the crown of the third molar forms in the period between early adolescence and approximately sixteen years. The chemistry of a thigh bone may, similarly, continue to develop into adolescence. And if organic material such as hair is preserved, we can see movements much closer to their time of death, as we shall see later in the book.[7]

So not only is our landscape inscribed into our skeleton; we are, to some extent, made of it.

So much for individuals. Even newer developments in the study of ancient DNA are revealing the movements of entire populations, and providing answers to debates that have raged for years. This is a tremendously exciting time to be an archaeologist.

PART 2

Treading

3. PRINTMAKING: WRITING ON THE EARTH

*In which we dodge elephant dung and discover
the earliest footprints*

It's not lost on me, the irony of writing about mobility while sitting at my desk for hours, with a bent spine and cramped stomach. My body won't allow it, so I go for walks.

Until recently I would go for lunchtime walks through a small wood on the top of the Chiltern Hills, on the edge of the south Oxfordshire village where I lived.

The woodland is rigidly and dramatically divided into two parts: the first two-thirds or so is beech and bluebell, and the rest, butting right up against this, is an entirely different world made up of much younger planted conifers,

such as larch and pine. The difference between these two elements within the same wood hit me every time: the beech packed with life and thick with understorey, the other hung with lichen and eerily silent. Even the light is different.

The path I took winds in and out among the trunks and through the horizontal layers of both old and new parts. I would keep going until the path reaches a farmer's field on a steep scarp with views to a distant horizon, the cooling towers of Didcot power station dominating the middle ground – great, grey landmarks that have since been demolished.

At this point the path loops back through the woodland towards home.

I walked to shake out my legs and unfurl my body, and to maintain a daily connection with the world outside. Walking rejuvenates me, and over the years it has proved useful for working through my thoughts. Sometimes I would record them in a small pocket notebook. At other times, I might stew over difficulties at work.

I've done that walk hundreds of times, in all weathers and in different seasons. Each time, the woodland changes its feel, sometimes a little and sometimes a lot. I came to know its sounds and smells, whether the ground was covered in bluebells, summer shade, dry leaves, or snow.

I don't go there any more, because I had to move away, but we have a special relationship, the path and me. Whether kicking up dust from sun-baked clay, or squelching into rain-soaked mud, my feet have left their mark on it, and the path, in turn, has got deeply inside me. I've been shaped by the thoughts, feelings and physical exercise it made possible.

Of course, I'm not alone in this. You too will have powerful relationships with the places you've moved through, as our forebears had.

*

Paths have always been there, because paths are what we use to connect time and space. They are primary; their form built into our brain and part of our origin myth. Consequently, we rarely think about *their* origins; how they formed and where they came from. When we walk down a path, as I did mine, we tend not to think about the stories embedded in them. But when we do think about it, a hidden history is revealed, and something of the experience of our predecessors comes alive to us. History books record the big events from the past, but most of us are from generations of ordinary folk; to understand a little of their lives we need to follow their footsteps. The written historical record can only tell us a limited amount about prehistory, the part of the past I have mainly studied; only archaeology can give us a fuller picture. By following ancient paths, we see the past more clearly.

*

Footprint tracks are a compelling way to 'see' past movement. We can relate to them more easily, I think, than to the typical archaeological discoveries of, say, sherds of pottery or flint flakes. Footprints are momentary; a snapshot of someone's life – often the actions of just a few seconds, recorded in the sediment. There's an immediacy to them, like the thumbprint on my brother's amphora, an instant connection to the past.

But footprints are one of the most fragile of archaeological remains, and difficult to spot. For them to form in the first place, the conditions need to be just right. The ground must be slightly moist and soft, but not too wet. Once a print is made it needs to be rapidly filled with a contrasting sediment to preserve it, one with a coarser grain, for example, washed over during the following winter, perhaps, or finer-grained and blown in; anything that is different and that seals it soon after. Then it needs to be buried under protective layers and remain undisturbed through centuries, or millennia, for us to find. Such conditions are not common, and ancient footprints are very rare.[1]

They are also difficult to understand. In many cases, ichnology (the study of footprint tracks and related traces, *ichnos* being the Greek for footprint) uses tracking experts, especially indigenous experts, to help decipher them. This is particularly fruitful at cave sites, some of which I will mention shortly. Those of us brought up in an industrialised society are accustomed to paved surfaces and lack the necessary skills to understand the evidence on soft ground. Where we see indecipherable palimpsests of prints, the indigenous tracker intuitively reads stories of individuals with distinctive ways of walking. Where we see chaos, the tracker sees order. Understanding the full potential of footprints requires both archaeological skill and a tracker's intuition.

Like the study of dinosaur tracks, with which ichnology is mostly associated, we can learn from the way the maker of the tracks moved. From the trails we can see the direction someone is travelling in, measure their stride (the length of a complete cycle from left foot back to left foot again) and the cadence (the timing of the footfall). When you run or walk fast, your footprints will be far apart; if you stroll, they will be close together.

The cadence is written into the earth like a sentence or a song.

By measuring the size of the printmaker's foot, we can make a guesstimate of their age, using modern comparative studies. We can glean a certain amount on their height based on foot size. It is more difficult to say anything about the sex of the footprint maker, because the overlap between men and women's feet is pretty significant. And we can get information and insight from the evidence that they walked barefoot or with footwear (and what that was).

A single footprint can tell us so much, but trails of footprints tell much more, illuminating the extended behaviour and activity of people about whom we otherwise know nothing: shifts in their speed and direction, changes of course to avoid things or to take advantage of something unexpected, as well as whether they're moving in groups or alone.

Group trails are better still, because – as with so much of the movement described in this book – the evidence from one individual can't be relied upon to tell us about the population as a whole.

Children are well represented in footprint tracks, as are, to a lesser extent, disabled people too, which is important because neither are particularly easy to recognise elsewhere from the archaeological record and so their experiences are often lost to us. Footprint trails tell the stories of otherwise invisible people.

These ephemeral traces of life sometimes go right back into our deep past. They can tell the expert on human evolution a lot about how our early ancestors moved, including when they started to walk upright. One such example, in fact one of the oldest, is among the most famous and important sites in the world.

You might imagine that the truly great archaeological discoveries are the result of careful, painstaking work. And they usually are. But sometimes the strangest and most unlikely of happenstance makes them for you.

Mary Leakey was one of the great archaeologists of the twentieth century. A descendant of the famous nineteenth-century antiquarian John Frere, she spent the 1950s and 1960s excavating at Olduvai Gorge in northern Tanzania with her husband Louis. The pair received global acclaim after discovering the bones of a 2-million-year-old human species. But Louis died in the early 1970s and Mary turned her attention to a different site: Laetoli, on the southern margin of the Serengeti plains. Fragments of another of our distant ancestors, *Australopithecus afarensis*, had already been found there. It was to provide Mary with the greatest discovery of her life – probably the greatest of the twentieth century.

In the summer of 1976, a visiting group of young scholars arrived for a tour of the site. And one day, perhaps because the sun was getting to them, or maybe just out of boredom, one of these visitors picked up a ball of elephant dung and hurled it at the others. The group retaliated with their own balls of dung. Dodging the incoming missiles, Yale University's Andrew Hill leapt and prostrated himself within a small gully. With his face almost touching the rocky surface he had a perfect ant's-eye view of the world. To his surprise he noticed curious indentations within a band of sediment that was eroding from the side of the gully. The game stopped and a closer inspection was made. They were ancient animal footprints fossilised within the deposit.

Mary Leakey and her team spent the next few years working in this area, slowly but surely uncovering more prints, millions of years old, from lumbering rhinos and stotting antelopes, right down to the little traces of marching millipedes. Even the tiny dents of pattering rain drops could be seen – the shortest imaginable moments in time, captured and fossilised. The prints are in what became known as 'footprint tuff', a hardened ash that has been dated to 3.66 million years ago and probably derived from the now extinct Sadiman volcano, some twenty kilometres away.

Exciting as this was, the team hoped for more: to find the footprints of one of our early ancestors.

And they did: unmistakable traces of human-like toes and heels. These footprints clearly showed an early human species, likely to be *Australopithecus afarensis*, walking tall on two extended legs, without crouching or using knuckles as support. If you have ever wondered what it's like to work as an archaeologist, you can imagine how thrilling this was.

The tracks belonged to three individuals of different body sizes – tall, medium, and small – possibly a family. The smaller one walked, limping, alongside the larger, while the middle-sized one walked behind, carefully and delicately stepping within the footprints of the tallest.

More recently, further tracks have been found, belonging to another group walking together on the same orientation as the previous trail, and at the same approximate speed. At over 3.5 million years old (that's more than 145,000 generations ago) this is the earliest evidence for fully bipedal humans in the world.[2]

Since writing that paragraph, I've been out for some fresh air, and walked considerably further than those fossilised tracks. It wasn't a particularly remarkable walk, not the kind of thing I would imagine putting in a book, but then, the walk that left those ancient traces may not have seemed important to them, either.

These footprints provide a beautiful echo of actions from a mind-bogglingly long time ago. They allow a study of foot anatomy, early human movement on two feet, and a tiny – frustratingly tiny – glimpse of early human behaviour. As Mary Leakey put it: 'This motion, so intensely human, transcends time.'

At Koobi Fora in Kenya, two distinct tracks of *Homo erectus* date from much more recently – a mere 1.52 million years ago. These too are accompanied by animal and bird tracks.[3]

Outside Africa, the oldest known footprints actually come from just next to a small village on the north Norfolk coast. The village name is spelt Happisburgh, but – and this is not uncommon for Norfolk – pronounced quite differently, as Haysbruh. These prints, dating to almost a million years ago, were made by an early ancestor, probably *Homo antecessor* ('Pioneer Man'), who somehow survived northern Europe's perishingly cold winters, much colder than they are now.

The Happisburgh prints are interesting because they show a family wandering along the edge of an estuary. Children's footprints meander like my own children's nearly a million years later: wandering, inquisitive and exploring. To think about the familiarity of this every-day action, almost certainly forgotten soon after by the printmakers themselves, but echoing down all those generations, never fails to move me.

In 2017, a life-size image of the Happisburgh footprint surface was projected onto the floor of the British Museum in London. At the time, I was working not a million miles away. The opportunity was just too tempting so I jumped on a train and headed to the capital to see them. Visitors were encouraged to step into the images, so I did. I carefully placed my feet on top of each projected print, following their walk, their precise line of direction. It gave me the same warm chill I had felt when I stood on the soles of Anthony Gormley's upside-down statue in Cambridge.

Racing forward in prehistory, footprints at Theopetra Cave in Thessaly, Greece, show two children, from 135,000 years ago, following each other. They were either Neanderthals or early *Homo sapiens*, but what really distinguishes them is that one was wearing a thin foot covering: the most ancient footwear known in the world. It's frustrating that we can't decipher the species from their prints alone. But the burning question that ran through my head as I read the scientific paper was: why did only one of them have shoes? The footprints themselves give no obvious and conclusive explanation.

Then there are the footprints at Le Rozel in Normandy, France, a mere 80,000 years old. These lack clear toe impressions, even on the really well-preserved prints, which make it likely that the Neanderthals who made them were also shod.

What else can footprints tell us? Well, the location itself can reveal something of people's lives, and culture.

A number of caves from the Romanian Carpathians have preserved the footprints of both Neanderthal and early *Homo sapiens* (and, alarmingly for them, cave bears) within a deposit known, rather romantically, as 'moonmilk'. At Tuc d'Audoubert Cave in Ariège, France, there are more than 300 footprints of late Pleistocene hunter-gatherers. These are found mainly along passageways associated with cave art, indicating people coming and going, as well as stopping to paint on the walls.

One of these tracks shows an individual losing their footing in the wet mud of the cave floor and then walking away very slowly – as indicated by the cadence of their prints – in a manner that will be familiar to anyone who has had a near miss like that. Others show people slipping and sliding so that they had to hold on to the side of the cave. Another bumped a foot on a rock, causing a stumble, while one less fortunate soul slipped so badly in the cave that they landed on their backside.

If only prehistoric swearing had somehow been recorded too.

Some prints show people walking bent over to get through the low passage, while others squatted or went on their knees. My own favourite of this collection of footprints shows a group of children very deliberately walking on their heels. Who doesn't remember doing that as a child?

Sometimes footprints tell us something about the tools people carried. At Willandra Lakes in Australia, footprint tracks along the edge of an ancient freshwater lake, dated to between 20,000 and 25,000 years ago, contain, among much else, evidence of a one-legged man and his support pole. In Italy two adults, an adolescent, and two children walked barefoot into Bàsura Cave some 14,000 years ago: the evidence demonstrates that they lit their way with a burning torch.

Earlier, we saw wandering in the Severn Estuary. Altogether, 21 distinct trails have now been recorded there, some of them leading to known and excavated Mesolithic hunter-gatherer campsites, some converging on points that (presumably) had once been similar sites, and others apparently leading to fish traps. Many of the printmakers are children, some as young as four, showing that even the young were venturing out into the muddy estuary and contributing to community life.

A similar network of visible human and animal trails has been recorded across the mudflats at Formby Point in north-west England. These trails are of a similar Mesolithic date, and again offer a snapshot of activity: people busying themselves along the edge of the sea, presumably fishing and collecting shellfish. Again, children were present. Most people were barefoot, but some had shoes. Memorably, one of the tracks was made by someone missing their second toe. How might that have happened? Was it an injury or a deformity? Like the Severn Estuary tracks, these footprints are a palimpsest of the small-scale movements by which people structure their everyday lives.

More than most other elements of archaeology, we 'get' footprints – we know the feeling of bare feet sinking into soft, wet mud and the sensation of it squeezing up through our toes, or the panic as one foot slides out from under us. Prints connect us with the printmakers. And these trails highlight what we miss in the archaeological record when we focus on Point A and Point B without considering what went between them. Travel is not reducible to the points of departure and arrival, as any epic tale in verse, or on film, confirms. The excitement is found in the journey.

4. FOOTFALL: WALKING AS PERFORMANCE

In which we see that, in every culture, there are right and wrong ways to move our feet

The scene is of two feet striking the street and hitting the beat. There is no body in the frame; the camera is focused only on the feet. It's all about the feet, in hand-made maroon-leather shoes, not so much walking as strutting. They have a rhythm and a groove.

In the background rises a rolling guitar riff before the unmistakable falsetto voice of Barry Gibb floats in. The camera pans up and we see a young man striding easy on a busy street. He steps smart with a suave, swinging swagger. High and light. Rolling. He has a hustle about him. A presence. An oozing confidence that claims the street and shouts: 'Look at me!'

His walk is his performance.

You may be familiar with this scene, from the opening credits of the 1977 film *Saturday Night Fever*, in which 23-year-old John Travolta strutted down Brooklyn's 86th Street to the beat of the Bee Gees' 'Stayin' Alive', and walked himself into movie stardom.

In archaeology, we tend to forget about people strutting like Travolta. Too often, we describe the movements of people in the past as if they were all, essentially, robots marching rationally and impassively across the landscape.

Having worked out a route people took, we make maps that resemble the opening credits of the television series *Dad's Army*, with long arrows pointing to where people came from and where they went to. But being able to demonstrate that people moved from here to there does not mean that we can understand what motivated that journey, or whether it was even intentional.

For good reasons, we look for rational explanations, so that our discussions frame movement as a cost and benefit, chosen logically. Mobility gets reduced to a sort of involuntary and behavioural reaction.[1] But the body is not a machine and we don't walk in a uniform, regular way across a flat and even surface. Movement is complex, unpredictable, and often socially driven. In our own lives, we walk, shuffle, run, climb, dawdle and dance. We pace, march, swing, dash, stroll, crawl, scramble, ramble, plod, hobble, trudge and tramp. Linger, loiter, saunter, wander and roam. And each of these kinds of movement gives off a different message to the bystander.

Other messages we might pass on through our walk include things like physical condition, age, or even just mood and emotional state. The vibrant energy of youth can be contrasted with the shuffling arthritic legs of old age, while a hobble may acknowledge a lifetime of hard work. A stooping trudge may be fatigue, or depression, or both. We walk differently depending on whether we are at the start or end of our journey (an actual one, or life's metaphorical trip). There are sporty runners and slow plodders. There are the pregnant, the overweight, the ill and the injured.[2]

Mobility has different meanings depending on who you are, where you are, and what sex you are. Coming across a stranger in an otherwise empty woodland engenders a different feeling than passing someone on a busy street. Someone walking uncomfortably close behind you on a street can feel threatening, depending on whether you (and they) are a man or woman, young or old.

The French sociologist Marcel Mauss pointed out that walking involves specific and culturally variable techniques of the body. People learn and practise additional techniques according to age, ethnicity, class, gender or sexual orientation. He gave as an example the practice of goose-stepping, then used by the German army to lengthen a soldier's stride, which sounds like a good idea but looked ridiculous to many people outside Germany. Movements are performed and practised in many ways, Mauss observed, some freely, others under restrictions; some requiring exertion, others easy. Some people and groups conform to socially acceptable mobility, and those who don't may be seen as needing to be controlled.

The nomadic Tuareg of the Sahara and Sahel have understood this better than most of us. Master trackers, they pride themselves on their ability to recognise specific individuals by their footprints. They know the distinctive, individual walk of everyone in their camp, as well as nearby ones, and can easily separate these footprints from those left by strangers. This way they know when an outsider has been around. Tellingly, they can often even determine who that outsider is, or at least what group they come from, by their distinctive tracks in the sand. Berbers, say the Tuareg, have a haughty, straight-backed, slow and steady walk, and this is reflected in the footprints they leave behind. The Wodaabe of Niger often walk with a stick since they travel a lot, and this is easily seen in the holes it leaves in the ground. People from lower artisan castes and former slaves are recognisable by their small, quick steps, and it is said that because they swing their arms negligently behind them their footprints are disordered and uneven. For these Tuareg trackers, the characteristic gait and pace of different groups, as seen in their tracks, tells them a whole host of things about who is on the move, not least their character. In effect, the Tuareg are practising a kind of archaeology of the very recent past.

In every culture there are the right and the wrong ways to walk: 'I knew a man who was arrested as a runaway lunatic,' noted Robert Louis Stevenson in his essay *Walking Tours*, 'because although a full-grown person with a red beard, he skipped as he went like a child.' This helps to explain why *Monty Python* audiences laughed so much at John Cleese's Ministry of Silly Walks.

Looking back, in interviews, Travolta described his swaggering dancer's walk as 'the walk of coolness'. An affected, carefully learnt walk from his school days in Brooklyn.[3]

The seventeenth-century poet and essayist Sir Thomas Overbury might not have recognised the specific walk used by Travolta, but Overbury knew his own version. In his writing he described an 'affectate traveller', dressed to seem French or Italian, 'and his gait cries, "Behold me".'

Mauss would have agreed, and gone further: all bodily movements vary according to cultural and local conventions, he wrote. The meaning is understood by the context. As culture can be expressed through clothes or art, so can it be expressed through the way individuals move.[4]

How is that transmitted? Most of us don't learn to move by reading a manual. We learn from the people around us. When I watch my daughters pace with their hands behind their back, I know that they have learnt that walk from me. And I have been told I walk like my father, although I cannot see it. Schoolchildren learn the latest 'cool' walk from their peers, à la John Travolta, and learn more 'formal' or 'sensible' walks from their teachers – though the specifics will vary according to whether you are in, say, Britain, Japan, or the Caribbean.[5]

If this is so today, can we assume it was the same in prehistory? Did *Homo erectus*, at Koobi Fora, have a cultural preference? Did *Homo sapiens* develop a walk of coolness to use in the event of a cave bear showing up? Did they strut their stuff in the Neolithic, or power walk in the Bronze Age? Presumably they did.

One of the great frustrations of archaeology is that we cannot always 'see' the individual, and we struggle to determine their thoughts. So we must rely on the written record to fill these gaps. Roman writers made much of the idea of walking as a performance. By their movement through the urban setting, Romans could advertise their status. 'We do not walk,' wrote the Roman philosopher Seneca, 'we parade.'[6] A person's style of walking provided an identity, separating the 'cultured' (Greek and Roman) from the barbarian other.

What kind of clues would watchers look for? Gait, obviously, which to Romans distinguished men from women, free men from slaves. Through contemporary texts and the people around them, young, free-born men learnt to walk the 'right way', not only to demonstrate their social status but in order to deserve it.[7] Speed was important too. Slaves ran, but aristocratic men didn't, because they wanted to reflect a cautious and considered persona. They didn't linger either, in case they appeared womanish.

As for Roman women: gait should be graceful, but not ostentatious. Ovid set out the extremes to avoid, in his poem *The Art of Love*. The dainty woman 'swings her sides artfully, taking in air with her flowing tunic, and she haughtily takes measured steps,' whereas the uncultured woman 'plods like the sunburned wife of an Umbrian farmer, and takes huge, straddling steps'. The ideal, for Ovid, lay somewhere between the two.[8]

We've already seen the connection between the movement of the feet and the movement of the mind, inspiring writers, thinkers and artists. Roman authors such as Seneca argued that an inconsistent gait equalled an inconsistent mind, whereas a confident step meant confident thought. The Tuareg would agree.

Like me with my daughters, the Romans recognised gait as something shared by families. In our own time, in these technological and security-conscious days, we can confirm this with 'gait analysis and recognition technology' alongside other biometric identification technologies, such as fingerprint, iris and voice recognition.[9]

*

So we are recognisable by the way we walk. Beyond individual gait, other factors have, throughout history, indicated wealth and status. Some Romans were carried in a litter by groups of bearers: a decadent form of travel that literally and metaphorically lifted them above the masses. Roman aristocrats further displayed their power through the retinue that walked with them. The larger its size, the more powerful they appeared, like a mafia boss surrounded by his henchmen, or a pop star with an entourage. Grouped movements like this conveyed the power to defend or threaten – an important political message, difficult to ignore.[10] Even more so: formal processions, such as those associated with triumphs, funerals and religious festivals. These could be merry, boisterous affairs, or penitential and full of self-reflection. They might be accompanied by singing and dancing, or mourning and weeping. Typically, just like today, they would follow specific pathways, in specific places.

Walking in the Roman world was a profoundly social activity; just as it still is in modern societies, and no doubt was in prehistory. Certain architectural features in the Roman villa provided settings for intellectual conversations, encouraging the movement of both body and mind. Outside, gardens were private spaces that choreographed movements through colonnaded walkways and garden paths, so that the householder could have ambling conversations with guests. The rhythm of walking shaping the rhythm of talking, and vice versa.

Where the Greek and Romans got those cultural practices is open to question, but we can see much the same in other periods afterwards.

Jumping forward in time, we find movement being choreographed in formal medieval and Renaissance 'pleasure' gardens. Set around castles and high-status residences, these carefully designed landscapes channelled people along a staged processional route, manipulating vistas so that one could be glimpsed after another. Views of the castle or residence were carefully revealed to the visitor, stage-by-stage, to create a spectacle.[11]

Using plane tables, measuring tapes and theodolites, archaeologists have surveyed and assessed the earthwork remains of the fifteenth-century pleasure garden known as the Pleasance at Kenilworth Castle, in Warwickshire.[12] They established that the principal approach to the Pleasance, for the lordly or royal visitor, was by boat or barge. Passengers would have been rewarded with staged prospects at several points on the journey: hidden and slowly revealed, slipping from view only to be seen again as they rounded each corner – tantalising, like a sort of striptease. For travellers on horse or on foot to Kenilworth, causeways focused movements along them, directing people as much as constraining them, while areas of water created further boundaries, as well as illusions, such as the reflection of certain well-chosen views.

As we will see in a later chapter, prehistoric monument complexes were arranged rather like this too, with individual monuments to be seen and hidden, glimpsed and covered, as you walked along their landscape. The traveller a player in a giant theatre.

Set apart from the humdrum activities of everyday life, formal gardens provided a different space to move around in. They were colourful, scenic, scented spaces designed to stimulate the body and the mind. Visitors could be met in them and conversations shared, or, if alone, they might be quiet places where you moved around in a similar way to, say, the cloisters of monasteries or universities – ambulatories designed for reading, meditating, or silent prayer: travelling with the feet, and further with the mind. The formal nature of these gardens, and the movement around them, had clear liturgical associations, not least an echo of the Garden of Eden, the ultimate idealised prehistoric landscape.

Pleasure gardens were also frequently associated with courtly love, and feature in the tales of Chaucer, the Arthurian stories of Thomas Malory, and the fourteenth-century romance *Sir Gawain and the Green Knight*.[13]

If this sounds like high culture, it was. To appreciate the complex meaning and symbolism of these gardens required courtly knowledge, and it separated the elite from the lower classes. Indeed, access was reserved for the select few.

The same can be said for the castle itself: movement around the castle, or any other high-status residence, was no less choreographed. Before even coming in, a visitor's status was displayed for all to see, because entry through the gates varied from person to person, depending on rank. High-status visitors would have the pleasure of seeing the gates thrown open wide in a grandiose expression of welcome. Others were obliged to enter through a wicket gate (a smaller door set within the gates), like modern hotel staff using a separate entrance. This might well involve stooping, as the archaeologist Matthew

Johnson points out – and thereby enforcing a bow to the lord as you crossed the threshold.[14]

Castles operated to an everyday rhythm, starting with the daily raising of the gates. Once inside, visitors would need to know the right behaviour, and know which areas were accessible to their sex and social rank at each stage of their progress towards the high-status rooms of the host. Should they be invited to dinner, status would be displayed by their position at the table – as at any modern wedding – and later by access (or not) to socially exclusive private rooms.

The bedchambers of later seventeenth-century palaces and large houses, such as Hampton Court, required visitors to progress through successive, increasingly private, areas; each one controlled by a series of checks. As long as the visitor kept passing through, their status was enhanced.[15] Gaining privileged access to the royal bedchamber was somewhat like, today, being fast-tracked through an airport; but having arrived at the inner sanctum, Johnson writes, visitors might be made to wait in a sometimes chilly waiting room (like queueing outdoors today, even when you hold a first-class ticket, on the steps of the plane). As we shall see later, immobilising people, and controlling their movement, is a time-honoured power trip.[16]

Separate and contrasting forms of movements existed for servants, though, who had direct access to the bedchamber via hidden backstairs, although they too will have had some form of social ranking. These backstairs formed a sort of dark mobility; clandestine movements that could allow hidden comings and goings, and could be used – indeed, at times were used – for secret and subversive liaisons.[17]

*

Throughout history, we find abundant evidence of another culturally specific movement: the promenade. Verbs such as 'to stroll' and 'to saunter', previously associated with vagabonds, acquired respectability from the eighteenth century onwards. The words retained an association with idleness, but this was welcome to aristocrats because it distinguished them from the industrious, busy middle classes.[18]

In nineteenth-century Paris, citizens promenaded along the boulevards and squares of Baron Haussmann's spectacular new city. These renovations were principally intended to allow a greater flow of traffic, as well as social control (they replaced the disease-ridden narrow streets of medieval Paris, which were a hotbed of crime and revolutionary turmoil), but they also redefined urban space.

Integral to Haussmann's work were new parks, linked by boulevards from the city. These were hugely popular. Both tourists and Parisians alike flocked to these new spaces, to strike poses and show off their clothes and sophisticated gait. Young dandies displayed their fine stockinged calves. Impressionist painters such as Manet, Degas and Renoir went on to document this social spectacle; and as new lighting technologies emerged, promenading at nighttime became popular too.[19]

*

I've leaned heavily on the written record in this chapter. It goes without saying that prehistoric life lacked electricity, boulevards and the music of the Bee Gees. But it's reasonable to suppose that things we have glimpsed in this chapter might have applied for as long as there have been human beings.

Take, for example, the concentric rings of wooden posts and standing stones erected in Britain and elsewhere at the end of the Neolithic period. These have been likened to circular mazes, with navigation as part of the ceremony. They are deceptively complex. Some were approached by miniature avenues of upright posts, forcing visitors into a single file, and once inside they did not just walk into the centre, but moved about in a complex manner. Offerings were placed against the posts, sometimes with differences between what was placed in the outer and innermost rings, or between different sectors of the monument.

This certainly seems to be the case at two monuments in Wiltshire: The Sanctuary, a circle of timber posts and standing stones near Avebury, and Woodhenge, six concentric ovals of standing posts surrounded by a bank and ditch near Stonehenge. Both were excavated by the redoubtable archaeologist Maud Cunnington between 1926 and 1930. A colossus in Wiltshire archaeology, Maud had already excavated many of the great monuments in the area, carefully writing up her findings and publishing the results. After finishing excavations at both Woodhenge and The Sanctuary, Maud, a strong believer in public archaeology, and her archaeologist husband Ben Cunnington (whose great-grandfather was the famous antiquarian William Cunnington), bought both sites and gave them to the nation. She was awarded a CBE for services to archaeology in 1948.

Using the results of Maud Cunnington's careful excavations, archaeologist Joshua Pollard was able to re-analyse both Woodhenge and The Sanctuary in the 1990s, and from this he identified the patterning of various artefacts, such as fragments of pottery, pieces of worked flint and antler, carved chalk objects, and even small bits of human bone, from the site. These indicate that people moved around these rings of stone and timber in an agreed, organised way, depositing specific offerings at the uprights as they went. People entering the monument were not able to make a direct line to the centre, but followed a circuitous path that led them around the concentric rings. At Woodhenge, handfuls of human bones were placed around posts at certain points, including on either side of the entrance, and in the centre was a burial of a child, two or three years old.[20] These monuments show a choreographed mobile performance, just like passing through the puzzle mazes found in formal pleasure gardens.

Historically, mazes and labyrinths have often been used in this way to represent a journey – either real, symbolising actual paths, or metaphorical enactments of life, death and rebirth. At Chartres Cathedral in France, a labyrinth on the floor, dating from the thirteenth century, symbolised a miniature pilgrimage to the Holy Land, providing a substitute for those who couldn't make the real journey.

Entering such a maze might change you: 'A walker leaving a labyrinth is not the same person who entered it,' writes Hermann Kern in *Through the Labyrinth*, 'but born again into a new phase or level of existence.'[21]

Were prehistoric monuments understood, and used, in this way too, standing in for longer journeys and pilgrimages? Narratives that were walked into being? Stories that were told with the feet? There's nothing to say that they weren't.

5. PATHMARKING:
LINES IN THE LANDSCAPE

In which footsteps become our tracks and trails, and a famous antiquarian names a monument

As we follow in our ancestors' footsteps, tracing their paths, we become part of a line of movement that is walked into existence by many feet, over long periods.

There is a difference, then, between footprints and paths, between ichnology and hodology (from the Greek *hodos*, meaning path). By studying footprints, we can glimpse fleeting moments in the lives of individuals. Paths tell us about whole communities, and behaviours that play out over generations.

Paths are maintained by use, through trampling the ground. This compacts the soil and damages anything that grows. Grazing animals, wild or domestic, push back vegetation and open the line of the path even further. Paths may need some seasonal work to maintain them, such as cutting the spring and summer growth, but regular use is generally enough.

Over long periods, paths become distinct ecosystems, quite different to the surrounding landscape. Seeds from animal droppings lead to particular plant communities growing up along trails. Humans add to this too, spitting out crab-apple pips or blackberry seeds as we go, tossing plum or sloe stones to the side as we walk. Or clumsily dipping into a pocketful of gathered hazelnuts and dropping one or two. Defecation along routes, human and animal, adds nutrients and further enhances linear occurrences of favourite food plants. People can more knowingly manage plants along paths, and those used for medicine, dye, fibre and string can be transplanted along routeways too, needing only small amounts of encouragement afterwards: the odd bit of pruning, burning, coppicing, harvesting, mulching and weeding on the move. In this way we create very particular environments along paths.[1] Next time you walk along a path, picking at blackberry bushes and crab-apple trees, think of the countless travellers who have been able (perhaps like you) to stave off hunger because of that path. Give a thought, too, to the generations of people over centuries past that have created these distinct linear environments that you use. We are almost entirely blind to these plants now, but their existence along paths is no coincidence. Know too that when a path is removed or widened by a landowner or the council, and the pathside vegetation destroyed, they are erasing hundreds, perhaps even thousands, of years of history.

So paths are formed by habit. They're manifestations of the routine and the everyday. They are mundane, humdrum – and, paradoxically, they're all the more exciting because of that. They exist because they're used and if they stop being used, they grow over and cease to exist. To stop them being lost, the people who moved on them developed systems of marking them.

One way, still familiar to us, is to mark trees along the route; cutting symbols into the trunks and removing patches of bark, or bending saplings in the direction of the path, a process known as trailblazing. We might think of a trailblazer as a pioneer in science, business or research, but a true trailblazer is a pathmarker; someone who follows paths and marks routes. Just as a horse is known by the distinctive white 'blaze' that runs down its face, so specific paths come to be known by the distinguishing blaze marked on pathside trees.

Routes can be marked in other ways too – through waymarkers and signposts – that send a message to the traveller. In Europe, later prehistoric routeways were likely to have been marked by cairns and other monuments, or symbols carved onto boulders, indicating the best routes, or the direction of significant or ceremonial places. In this way, long lines of Bronze Age burial mounds, known as round barrows, indicate so-called 'barrow roads' across Europe. The original path itself having been lost, only the lines of barrows remain for us to see.[2]

*

Not all routes require marking; some are held in memory. In the arid lands of central and southern Arizona in the US and northern Sonora in Mexico, long routes are expressed during song performances known as song cycles. The songs represent actual trails and are sometimes told in real time, even if that means singing them through the night. They identify landmarks – a specific sand dune or hill – and through them people learn how to get around.

These song cycles can be symbolic, sacred or narrative accounts of ancestral journeys. In his book *The Songlines*, Bruce Chatwin beautifully describes the journeys of ancestral beings, given voice in the endless aboriginal Dreamtime of Australia.[3]

In Britain, a type of Neolithic monument known as a cursus has been identified as potentially marking out a similar spiritual or otherworldly path. Cursus monuments, dating from between 3500 BCE and 3000 BCE, are long, thin earthen avenues with edges defined by parallel ditches and banks, or by lines of pits and large postholes dug into the ground. They are mysterious. They seem to mark out a straight track or routeway, but intriguingly they have closed, square ends: they are not throughways, but very long enclosures. They were named by the remarkable eighteenth-century antiquarian William Stukeley, who was the first to recognise this type of monument within the Stonehenge landscape.

A Lincolnshire doctor-turned-clergyman, and arguably England's most famous antiquarian, Stukeley had a particular genius for observing and drawing prehistoric landscapes, with both artistic ability and a surveyor's accuracy. He had an eye for the complete countryside, rather than individual monuments, and many of his astute observations of landscapes are still used by archaeologists today.

But his illustrations are not flawless. He had a habit of going back to his early manuscripts and drawings of the 1720s, and altering them to fit in with his later interpretations. He did this especially to drawings of the monuments around Avebury henge, a monument we will come to shortly. As Stukeley became increasingly devout, he began to see prehistoric monuments as embodiments and reflections of early Christian iconography. He manipulated his early accurate drawings to fit better with these interpretations. He did something similar with the Stonehenge cursus, which he had originally drawn, rightly, as having square ends, but later convinced himself that it was a Roman chariot racetrack and redrew it with a curving arch at the end, like the Circus Maximus in Rome.[4] He named it, and therefore this whole class of monument, 'cursus', after the Latin for 'movement'. The name suits it well, I think, even if it was built on misidentification and falsification.

Today, more than 100 cursus monuments have been identified across Britain and Ireland. Some are a few hundred metres long; others extend several kilometres across the landscape. The biggest, the Dorset Cursus, is almost ten kilometres long, running in a crooked line across the chalk downland of Cranborne Chase, from Martin Down at its north-eastern end to Thickthorn Down at its south-western. Cursuses are among the very largest monuments in prehistory and represent the sum of immense labour. Most have been ploughed away and become difficult to see on the ground: you really need to view them from above to see them properly. What were they for?

Current interpretations cover a range of practical and spiritual functions: marking and monumentalising pre-existing paths, cosmological alignments, assembly points on long-distance cattle-moving routes, marking out metaphorical routes for rites of passage, ceremonial processions, or ritualised forms of pilgrimage. Did people walk within these vast monuments in silence? Perhaps they sang, or chanted, or danced? Maybe they didn't walk *inside* them at all, but alongside, so that the spirits of the recently dead, or the long dead, could walk in procession within.[5]

Quite honestly you can let your imagination run wild, because there is little in the way of artefacts from cursus monuments to contradict you. This is one of the great joys and frustrations of archaeology: to give free rein to the imagination, in order to understand the past, and then to set those fancies alongside the evidence, and keep only what fits.

Henges were constructed slightly later than cursus monuments, and continued from the Neolithic into the Bronze Age. They are again earthen enclosures, but this time circular in shape, defined by a bank with an inner ditch. Henges may well have been used as gathering places for a largely pastoral society, where people came together at certain times of the year for feasting and to exchange objects, news and ideas. But they were also likely religious centres, on the evidence of the sorts of precious artefacts we find in them: the henge as a hierophany, a manifestation of the divine, from the Greek *hieros* ('holy') and *phainein* ('to reveal'). They take their name from Stonehenge which, confusingly, isn't – under our modern definition – a true henge.

Some henges have two opposing entrances, pointing to a line of movement: into, through and out. This gives us a sense that these numinous monuments may have been strung out along existing paths, their entrances both physically and symbolically sending the traveller along the course of their journey. These alignments were sometimes followed, later, by Roman and medieval roads, adding weight to this argument and showing that the route remained viable long after the monument itself had fallen out of use. Henges with four opposing entrances may therefore mark the crossroads of two routes.[6]

I have spent years trying to understand henges, and have excavated a few to get answers. My favourite is a monument we've already met: Marden henge, in the Vale of Pewsey in Wiltshire, midway between Stonehenge and Avebury. Half a kilometre long, from one end to the other, it is the largest in the country, earning it the elite title of megahenge. I excavated a series of archaeological trenches within it, over four wonderful summer seasons: despite its size, Marden is one of the least known of the big Wessex henges. Most attention has been within the Avebury area to the north, or that of Stonehenge to the south – both within a UNESCO World Heritage Site. Marden, in the middle, had been left out. Ever drawn to the underdog, I wanted to redress the balance, and get closer to understanding the meaning of these inscrutable monuments.

One of the most intriguing aspects of Marden henge is its position right on the River Avon. It has two opposing entrances and if we draw a route between them, it follows the river. Continue this route beyond the henge, south along the river for a few more kilometres, and we get to another huge henge, Durrington Walls. This other megahenge has also been recently excavated, showing a solid gravel routeway running from the river to one of its entrances. Again, it is clearly linked to the river.

If we continue our journey downstream we arrive at Stonehenge, which again has a large avenue linking it to the river.

I'm not sure I got very close to understanding what henges were for, although we did find some wonderful things during our seasons excavating in Marden, from Neolithic houses to the well-preserved remains of a feast. But I did get a strong sense that these three major monuments at least were all linked to the river and that a route flowed between them. Perhaps they were interconnected religious centres and people travelled between them as part of a prehistoric pilgrimage. Or were they more profane than that? Possibly, though it's hard to imagine that to journey between them was as humdrum as a daily commute.

There are other strings of henges around the country; their opposed entrances lining up so that it looks as if a path should link them up like beads on a necklace. One such string of henges, along a north–south corridor through the Vales of York and Mowbray in North Yorkshire, has been interpreted as part of a long-distance passageway, the 'Great North Route'.[7] This was subsequently followed closely by a major Roman road known as Dere Street. Today, that route is still in use, known by a rather more prosaic name: the A1(M).

Some henges and stone circles were approached by avenues flanked by stones, in the same way that some timber circles were entered by timber avenues. The best-known is Avebury, which had two great stone avenues leading to and away from it, the Beckhampton and West Kennet Avenues. These are thought to be grand processional routes into and out of the henge interior. Stukeley saw them as representing a serpent's body winding around the Neolithic mound of Silbury Hill. The serpent's head was, he believed, The Sanctuary, a monument we met in the last chapter, and he tweaked his survey to make it look more elongated and snakelike.

Henges, timber and stone circles, and other late Neolithic monuments could be said to be 'thin' places, where the veil between this world and the eternal one becomes translucent and gossamer-like, and to which distant communities travelled, using specific routes and at certain times of the year. On entering them, people moved around in prescribed and formalised ways, depositing symbolically charged artefacts and offerings. To me, they clearly had a role in religion and the supernatural. So are they evidence for prehistoric pilgrimage?

Whatever the truth of the matter, the thing that most strikes me about monuments like Avebury, Marden and Stonehenge is that, unlike footprints, they have been starkly visible to so many generations before us – all gazing on them as we do now, and sharing much of our desire to understand them.

6. PILGRIM:
MOVED BY THE SPIRIT

*In which we see the journey as more than the sum
of its parts, and discover the original holiday*

The figure of the pilgrim provides an archetypal image of someone on the move, and pilgrimage was a significant reason for journeying in the past. And that continues in the present.

A pilgrimage, as we've just seen, is characterised by movement, sometimes formalised, to and from sacred places that serve a wider community. It's not an everyday movement like hunting, gathering or commuting. It's a special occasion, generally planned well in advance. And it's a round trip: to a special destination, then back again. As such, it tends to be a movement between states of being, both physical and spiritual. In that sense every part of the trip has heightened significance.

The phenomenon is found almost universally across cultures and through time, and in nearly all religions, as well as in secular settings. How else to describe, for example, the yearly routine many people observe of travelling to music festivals such as Glastonbury? Looking back on our time from the distant future, archaeologists may wonder at the mountains of campsite material and music-related souvenirs buried in landfill nearby, just as we today find evidence of previous pilgrimage in the discarded materials of long-dead pilgrims.

Over the centuries of written history, millions of people have set out every year to undertake a pilgrimage in one form or another, whether Catholics to Lourdes, or Muslims to Mecca and Medina for the annual *hajj*. Thousands of walkers have followed the Camino, the pilgrims' path across Europe to the cathedral at Santiago de Compostela on the north-west coast of Spain, now a World Heritage Site.

In Japan huge numbers of people, wearing white shrouds and carrying pilgrims' staffs, head out on foot, by car or bus to take in 88 Buddhist temples on a 1,400-kilometre circuit of the island of Shikoku. And today pilgrimage is still responsible for the world's largest human gathering: the Kumbh Mela in Allahabad in India, which attracts some 100 million people. Held every three years, the ceremony focuses on ritual bathing where the sacred rivers, the Ganges and the Yamuna, meet.

*

For many people, the appeal of a pilgrimage is in the journey, as much as the start and end points. I can understand that. Though not religious, I've often contemplated taking one of the large pilgrimages. Many of the people who walk the Camino de Santiago are avowedly non-religious. Which leads us to ask: what motivates that?

Looking back, I realise that I did a kind of pilgrimage, years ago. My younger brother, Justin, and I decided to mark the tenth anniversary of our mother's death by walking 100 miles over five days from the house our grandmother once lived in, just outside Bath in Somerset, to our aunt's house in Devon. Obviously, the journey would be meaningless to anyone except us and our family, but at the time we did call it a pilgrimage. Really it was a walk of reflection. And here I think lies something important. Walking is a chance to reflect. A pilgrimage, however you want to define it, reveals the human condition of restlessness. But it also shows the desire to seek, not necessarily enlightenment, but something of the meaning of life through the journey. And walking in groups, in the way we have seen countless humans do throughout time, knits together relationships between people, and with places, things, feelings, and beliefs. In other words: everything that matters to us.

*

In European Christianity, pilgrimage is an act of religious devotion to God or a saint, a *peregrinatio pro amore Dei*, and people travel to holy sites such as monasteries and cathedrals. Pilgrimage sites become holy for other reasons too. Usually this is due to perceived supernatural qualities, and for Christians this is commonly linked to apparitions of the Virgin Mary. In 1061, during the reign of Edward the Confessor, Richeldis – the widowed wife of the lord of the manor of Walsingham Parva in Norfolk – three times had a vision of the Virgin Mary who told her to build, in Norfolk, a replica of Jesus' family house at Nazareth. After it was built, news of the apparition and of the Holy House spread, as did stories that illnesses could be healed by drinking water from its nearby wells. Walsingham became the centre of a Marian cult and developed into one of the most prominent English pilgrimage sites, visited by royalty.

This is not so different to the more recent development of Lourdes in southern France. In 1858 a teenage girl, Bernadette Soubirous, claimed to have had a series of visions of the Virgin Mary who revealed to her a spring. Rumours quickly spread of this vision and that imbibing the water could cure illness. With Church support it was declared an official Catholic pilgrimage site, transforming Lourdes into one of the world's most famous modern-day pilgrimage destinations, still receiving some 6 million visitors a year.

Other stories of apparitions include the village of Knock in Ireland, which in 1879 became a national pilgrimage site after a number of the villagers had visions of the Virgin Mary next to their local chapel. A similar vision in the 1980s in Medjugorje in Herzegovina led to Catholics flocking there too.

*

Turning to secular life, Elvis Presley's house Graceland, in Memphis, Tennessee has over recent decades been a destination for millions who describe themselves as pilgrims. They leave offerings and messages to 'the King' at Graceland's gates and at his grave. Interestingly, many people have claimed to enjoy visions of Elvis, at Graceland and elsewhere – sightings of the one they worship.

As well as visions, people travel to the location of physical remains, and this too applies to the secular sphere. During the strictly atheistic Soviet era in Russia,

Lenin's tomb and mausoleum in Moscow became a place of public reverence and pilgrimage. Millions travelled to Red Square to file in long queues past his embalmed body, much as they did in London in 2022 following the death of Queen Elizabeth II.

In doing so, they were following a longstanding practice found in the written history of many religious traditions – and there's no reason to suppose the practice doesn't go much further back into prehistory.

The presence of a saint's tomb, or of sacred relics, has historically provided a big draw to pilgrims. Relics could include the purported physical traces of a saint, such as their bones or other parts of their body, or items associated with their lives and their suffering. The tears or breast milk of Mary were coveted possessions for religious houses. Pieces from Jesus' life were supreme relics and much sought after. These included nails or pieces of wood allegedly from the cross he was crucified on, or sometimes literally a part of him. His foreskin was in particular demand – the Holy Prepuce as it was known – and at least 31 places across medieval Europe claimed to have the one and only Holy Foreskin.

There was, and for many still is, a belief that these items are alive with holy and spiritual power, and therefore worth journeying great distances to see.

So important were sacred relics to attracting pilgrims (and their money) that medieval monasteries and cathedrals competed ruthlessly with one another. After all, a good relic could put your town on the map. A thriving market in relics developed, and professional relic dealers (and swindlers) traded in items for huge sums of money.

Theft was common too, and some people would go to great lengths to secure a desired relic. One story tells that around 1190, Hugh, Bishop of Lincoln, while staying as a guest at Fécamp Abbey in Upper Normandy, was shown by monks the mummified arm of Mary Magdalene. Bending forward to kiss the relic, Hugh grabbed the arm from them and tried to break a piece off. Unable to do so, he put the hand in his mouth and, using first his front teeth and then his back, tried to bite off a finger. With the monks howling 'For shame, for shame!', he was eventually successful in tearing off two slivers, which he took back to Lincoln. There he was lauded for his initiative and later canonised.

Many pilgrimage centres focus around such relics. The best known is Santiago, which is said to hold the relics of St James the apostle and martyr. The Basilica of St Anthony in Padua in Italy contains the tomb of the saint. It also contains his tongue, which is kept in a reliquary. Pilgrims are still drawn to the basilica to see this relic, and in the shop one can buy pieces of muslin cloth that have been sacralised by being passed over it. In a similar way, the Temple of the Tooth in Kandy, Sri Lanka, attracts huge numbers of Buddhist devotees to see Buddha's dental relic.

*

As well as an act of religious devotion, pilgrimage is, and has always been, of cultural and social significance, and to some extent it is a performance to be read by others.[1]

Around the world, people put on special clothing for pilgrimages. This may have had a practical function, but it also served to show their intentions. Today, travellers to music festivals stand out from the crowd at train stations with their T-shirts acquired at previous events, wellington boots, and heavy rucksacks. In the medieval world their counterparts might have carried a long walking staff with a metal ferrule at the end, a mendicant's pouch for alms, a broad-brimmed hat, sometimes folded up at the front, and a long, coarse cloak. These items might well have been blessed at Mass before the journey started.

A fifteenth- or sixteenth-century burial within Worcester Cathedral Priory may provide rare evidence of a pilgrim. Still preserved were his knee-length boots, which were well-worn and had clearly covered some mileage. But the real indicator was that he was buried with his wooden walking staff, which had been painted purple (an expensive colour for the time). The staff had a cockle shell attached to it, which may indicate a pilgrimage he had undertaken to the shrine of St James at Santiago de Compostela.[2] In fact, it was quite common for medieval pilgrims to display evidence of previous journeys, and a scallop shell – or an image of one – also indicated that they had been to Santiago.

Other shrines provided tokens for pilgrims to display: little metal reliefs, known as pilgrim badges, depicting religious iconography, such as the shrine, church or other sacred place they came from. They were decorated on only one side so that they could be fastened with a pin or stitched on to a hat, cloak or bag. Cheap and mass-produced, they were souvenirs of pilgrimages past that could be proudly displayed for others to see. They were considered powerful objects too, full of religious potency thought to heal and protect the wearer.

Ampullae served a similar function. These were like pilgrim badges, but were little lead or pewter phials that held holy water, oil or liquid of some sort, and were usually attached to cord and worn as a necklace. A sealed ampulla found in Yorkshire contained an infusion of aromatic herbs and spices. Canterbury became a huge pilgrimage centre after the murder of Thomas Becket in 1170, attracting some 20,000 pilgrims a year at its peak. From here, visitors might take away ampullae containing holy water supposedly mixed with a tincture of Becket's blood. Known as 'Becket Water' or 'Canterbury Water', it was a sort of divine medieval homoeopathic remedy to cure all ills. The great medieval traveller and chronicler Gerald of Wales describes visiting the Bishop of Winchester in Southwark with an ampulla from Canterbury tied around his neck, and recorded that the bishop instantly recognised what it was, and where he'd been. He had read the code, in other words: it was the badge of the Canterbury pilgrim.

Archaeological evidence for these sacred travels comes mainly from the pilgrim badges, ampullae and scallop shells that have been found in burials and elsewhere. Large numbers turn up at river crossings in Canterbury and Salisbury, and even greater quantities along the Thames foreshore in London, testament to the flocks of returning pilgrims. Most are from local or national shrines, although at Salisbury excavated pilgrim badges of St Hubert and St Josse are likely to have originated from shrines in the Ardennes in Belgium and Picardy in France. At Meols, a village on the northern coast of the Wirral peninsula in England, seven pilgrim signs were discovered: three from

Santiago, one from Rome, two possibly from Aachen in Germany, and one from Our Lady of Rocamadour in France, indicating distant pilgrim travels.[3]

*

Medieval pilgrims were a varied bunch, and there were almost as many as there were motivations for pilgrimages. Some were undertaken voluntarily, to bear witness to faith and devotion. For others it was a way of life: people perpetually moving, a bit like a sadhu in Nepal or India. Others undertook a pilgrimage to earn an indulgence to reduce time in Purgatory in the afterlife (Gerald of Wales calculated that he had reduced his time by exactly 100 years). Many sought miraculous cures from disease, or relief from chronic pain, or to intercede for a sick friend or relative. As we've seen, Walsingham in Norfolk was purportedly a healing site and consequently became one of the leading pilgrimage destinations. Others desired protection – pregnant women, for example, hoping for a safe delivery for both mother and child. At the extreme end of the scale, some people made clear their devotion, and their share in Christ's humility, by starving themselves on the journey, or travelling barefoot, or even in fetters – heavy iron manacles around the ankles normally associated with the enslaved or imprisoned – deliberately and willingly making the experience more painful by bruising, blistering and injuring their feet.

Some pilgrims wanted none of that and were simply interested in getting together with a group of friends and neighbours to enjoy the experience of going somewhere, either as a day out, or for a longer trip. This would occur at specific times of the year to coincide with religious festivals and the fairs that often accompanied them. At Salisbury Cathedral in the twelfth century, for instance, a fair coincided with the Feast of the Nativity and the Feast of Relics in September, and great numbers of people were drawn to it. Likewise, an Easter fair of national importance developed around the healing spring and shrine of St Ivo, purportedly a Persian bishop who died as a hermit at Slepe near Huntingdon. We can see these more playful and recreational aspects in the ribald tales of people eating and drinking well in Chaucer's fourteenth-century *Canterbury Tales*. These holy days were the original holidays, and we find echoes of them in the circuses and travelling rides that provide seasonal recreation today, such as Winter Wonderland in Hyde Park.

It's remarkable to consider the contrast between this gaiety and the despair that hung over many pilgrims. Groups of merry-making youngsters would share a route with devout ascetics as well as the impoverished, the sick and the dying. But entertainment and tourism have always been elements of pilgrimage, and still are.

*

Another distinction between pilgrims was gender. Men could travel alone; women needed an escort, as well as permission from their legal guardian: a father for the unmarried, or otherwise a husband. Some shrines were restricted to men: women were prohibited to approach St Cuthbert's shrine in Durham Cathedral, for example, and relics or images in Carthusian or Cistercian houses were generally not accessible to women. There was also a heavy restriction on the mobility of nuns and other religious women in the late thirteenth and early fourteenth centuries, and nuns had to have the permission of their abbesses, which was rarely granted.[4]

And as in so much else, there was a social hierarchy. People with money had a better chance of getting close to a saint's shrine, and better transport. The pilgrim protagonists of *The Canterbury Tales* all had mounts. The pilgrim burial in Worcester Cathedral Priory mentioned above suggests a man of reasonable means, and the location of his burial site, inside the cathedral, confirms this.

The wealthy could buy pilgrim badges made of precious metals, rather than the cheap base metals available to most. Records show that two Dukes of Burgundy – Philip the Good and Charles the Bold – purchased gold and silver badges, as did Charles VIII of France. Those with money could travel to the Holy Land, Spain or Rome; Chaucer's Wife of Bath had 'thrice been to Jerusalem' as well as Rome, Santiago, Cologne and Boulogne. Those of humbler means would undertake only a short journey to a local or regional shrine. But generally, the pilgrim road itself was shared by rich and poor alike, and the two often rubbed shoulders.

Many records show that the wealthy paid others to go on pilgrimage for them – a kind of virtual travel. One such motionless pilgrim was the French countess Mahaut of Artois, who paid a pilgrim to visit Santiago on her behalf in 1304. Elizabeth of York sent two men on pilgrimages to various shrines in England in 1502: one visited Reading, Hales, Worcester and Walsingham, and the other Canterbury and London. Not too dissimilar,

I suppose, to people going on virtual pilgrimages now-adays, and 'visiting' pilgrimage sites vicariously on the internet (it's a real thing, you can look it up).

Often these paid pilgrimages took place after the death of the person who paid, as evidenced in their wills. Many stipulate that an honest man of good character should do the deed, providing money for travel, board and a daily wage. Edward Storey, Bishop of Winchester, left five marks in his will in 1502 so that his chaplain could go on a number of pilgrimages for him after his death, including to Canterbury. The Earl of Arundel, dying at home after the siege of Harfleur in 1415, likewise requested a pilgrimage to Canterbury be made for him – specifically, on foot.[5]

*

As pilgrims moved through the landscape, they influenced and affected the world around them. Offerings at shrines and the purchase of pilgrim tokens were an important source of income to the Church, in whose interest it was to encourage more pilgrims. We've seen how relics, and the pilgrims drawn to them, can transform a place. In the nineteenth century, the springs at Lourdes brought huge wealth and opportunities for entrepreneurs to sell kitsch souvenirs and trinkets, postcards and even sweets, known as Pastilles de Lourdes, made from the healing water. A new rail line was constructed to link Lourdes with Paris and beyond, and today water in plastic Virgin Mary bottles is shipped around the world.

In the medieval world, as now, the creation of a pilgrimage centre and the wealth it brought meant improved access, such as better roads, the benefits of which went beyond pilgrims to others on the move. Flourishing pilgrim traffic led to an increase in pedlars, traders and vendors, as well as taverns, hospices and lodgings along the pilgrim routes, so that others travelling them also benefited. Pilgrim fairs brought with them dance and theatre troupes, and Thames ferrymen did well by serving pilgrims travelling from East Anglia and Essex to Canterbury. No doubt criminals can be added to those who benefited from the large gatherings of people.

Being on the road, away from home, gave pilgrims great freedom, and that inevitably led them into temptations, counter to Christian morality. A nod to this comes from medieval erotic badges, rare in Britain but found in the archaeological record around Europe, that satirise the pilgrim badges we saw earlier. These explicitly, imaginatively, and sometimes magnificently, depict male and female genitalia – phalluses with wings or with legs and feet, or vulvas dressed up as little pilgrims complete with staff and hat. Sometimes couples are shown making love, other times they are lying legs akimbo. They are even shown dancing around giant phallus trees. In others, women sit on wandering phallus beasts, or push them in wheelbarrows. Basically, if you can think of it, there's a medieval badge depicting it. The internet, it turns out, is not responsible for our most morally bankrupt and niche desires: we've always been like that. We know almost nothing about where these items came from, but they were probably sold at the carnivals and fairs that accompanied religious festivals, and they hint that sexual freedom was, for some at least, part of the pilgrim experience. To counter this, the Church provided ample warnings along pilgrimage routes, mainly in the form of paintings in buildings, reminding pilgrims that sinners would receive divine punishment in the afterlife, often meted out on their genitalia.

Some had their punishment in this life. Pilgrimage was foisted on them by bishops as penance for misdemeanours and offences carried out at home: adultery, slander, heresy and more. These 'forced' pilgrimages might require the penitent to go to a particular cathedral and stand before the high altar with a candle during Mass, or to go barefoot, or even semi-naked. A certain naughty William Covel, to take an example, was found guilty of repeated adultery in the fourteenth century and commanded to go to Canterbury barefoot and bare-chested too, wearing only his trousers. And a man named John Mayde, guilty of adultery with his godmother, was sent on a pilgrimage to Santiago in 1325, which sounds a better deal to me.[6] The record doesn't show whether he did actually go, or how, on his return, he was able to prove that he had fulfilled his punishment. By producing a scallop shell perhaps, or a certificate of pilgrimage. Those convicted of heresy often had to wear yellow crosses on their front and back. For the more serious crime of murder, the convict would be made to hang the murder weapon around their neck for the duration of the pilgrimage. In all these cases, it was clearly much more about public humiliation than a religious experience. This was the pilgrimage as a walk of shame.

In the next chapter, we'll see more about how people in authority have used their power to enforce movement – and prevent it.

7. OVERSTEPPING: RESTRICTION AND RESISTANCE

In which we see the countryside change, and the origins of the mob

It's not quite the same as a pilgrimage, but most archaeologists I know take holidays designed around archaeological sites. I've yet to meet one who is satisfied to sit on the beach for two weeks without (at least) a brief visit to the local museum, church or castle. Many actually take time off work to go and dig on other people's sites. We do it during our working week, and then we go away and do it some more, just for the heck of it. It's part of our fabric.

This certainly applies to me. I love visiting archaeological sites when I'm on holiday, and each of them has a different feeling, producing distinct emotions. Stonehenge is a majestic heap of stones and a visit is rightly on many people's bucket list. Personally, I find it so busy as to be manic, with its crowds of day trippers, shuttle buses and gift shop with English Heritage tea towels and Stonehenge snow globes (obviously I have both).

At the other end of the spectrum is Wharram Percy, perched remotely on the side of the Yorkshire Wolds. It is a quiet site that gets few visitors. The archaeology is mainly lumps and bumps in pasture fields, and there is no visitor centre or toilets. Once a bustling medieval village, it thrived for around 600 years until it was deserted sometime around 1500. Unlike the modern vibrancy of Stonehenge, it is, for me anyway, a landscape of lament.

A visit was always on my itinerary when I holidayed in Yorkshire – that is, before circumstances drew me north more permanently. It is highly atmospheric, and the visitor can walk down what was once the main road of the village, and see grassed-over remains of around 40 abandoned houses, home to perhaps 200 people in its heyday. Some doorways are still visible as gaps in the earthworks. In these buildings entire lives played out. Babies took their first steps. Adults had blazing fireside arguments as well as moments of head-back, mouth-open, contagious laughter. Beyond them is the church, ruined now but still partly upstanding. Here, every Sunday, priests read sermons, choirs sang. In the fields nearby, animals grazed, farmers harvested. The millpond once shimmered with fish, to feed the manor on Fridays. Along the lanes children chased balls, or one another, or idly sat and pulled buzz-bones (bones threaded onto twisted cord that spin and hum when the ends are pulled), made up fantasy games with peg dolls, or threw dice and moved gaming pieces around a board. (All these pastimes have been found in excavations at Wharram Percy.) Along these same lanes, friends met, love grew, and gossip spread.

The aristocratic Percy family had a manor house here, but to mention that can mislead, because this is a place of everyday working people leading ordinary lives.

Our understanding of Wharram Percy is entirely due to the work of one man. In 1948, not long after becoming a lecturer in economic history at the University of Leeds, the large and somewhat shabby figure of Maurice Beresford stood in a field and looked at the isolated church and the mounds and hollows at Wharram Percy, and wondered about it all. He had seen something similar three years earlier at Bittesby in Leicestershire, and realised that he was looking at the remains of a deserted medieval village. This insight was followed by the recognition of hundreds of other deserted villages in England, and started his long and successful academic career.

Born in 1920, Beresford excelled at his grammar school and was accepted to study history at the University of Cambridge. A lifelong socialist and a conscientious objector during the Second World War, he had an innate feeling for both geography and history in the landscape. And for people: he had a lifetime's interest in human welfare, particularly that of prisoners, and he taught young offenders, even inviting them to excavate with him.

Beresford headed out to Wharram Percy over a few summer weekends in 1950 with some of his friends (he didn't drive and so needed people to ferry him around) along with a handful of students, spades and buckets. He confirmed his theory by chasing walls* and exposing house foundations, as well as retrieving pottery and other artefacts. A few years later, in 1954, *The Lost Villages of England* was published, setting out his thoughts and research; a seminal book.

....

* Archaeological speak for finding a section of wall in your excavation trench and then just following it until the whole building is revealed.

Beresford's small, and by his own admission, crude excavations in 1950 were the start of a research project that finally concluded in 1990. Digs took place for three weeks each summer for 40 years, and in total they excavated just under 10 per cent of the whole settlement. This might not seem a lot, but it was a pioneering project, using many of the techniques that archaeologists now take for granted, from big, open-area excavations to multi-disciplinarity, to geophysical and aerial survey work and environmental sampling. Beresford, who died in 2005, transformed our views of the countryside.

Through the work at Wharram Percy, we can piece together its history and ultimate demise. Successive bouts of the plague in the fourteenth century, as well as occasional Scottish raiding, reduced the size of the village, and it never fully recovered. But what really did for Wharram Percy was a process known as enclosure. This was prolonged and varied, and can be seen across large swathes of the countryside, but essentially it involved the taking back and parcelling up by individual landowners of open fields: large spaces made up of long, thin strips of cultivated land called selions, or ridges, that were distributed among the farmers of the village, who had traditional rights to work them. The same thing happened to commons, which are described below. Documentary evidence, confirmed by the archaeology, shows that evictions took place at Wharram Percy throughout the last decades of the fifteenth century. Records shown to the Commissions of Enquiry provide evidence for the eviction of four families and the deliberate destruction of their houses. Essentially, the (by now) absentee landlord served notice on tenants, then pulled down the homes. The last families were removed around 1500. Intriguingly, some pottery sherds of a slightly later date, as well as one or two sixteenth-century jettons (coin-like tokens), have been excavated from Wharram. We'll come back to these at the end of the chapter.

This happened – piecemeal and over time – in many places up and down the country. Throughout the fifteenth and sixteenth centuries, declining villages across rural England were finally emptied by landlords, evicting tenants and turning the now enclosed land over to sheep, which had become much more profitable due to the high price of wool.*

Beresford's work identified at least 1,300 similar places. Bordesley in north Warwickshire was totally enclosed by around 1500, while Middle Ditchford in Gloucestershire was abandoned slightly earlier, in the 1480s. Little Oxendon in Northamptonshire is another well-preserved deserted village, like Wharram Percy, with the main street visible down the middle of it, and on either side the remains of tofts and crofts (the house plots and attached strips of land). Beyond them are long, medieval plough lines, known as ridge and furrow. The whole place is now a series of humps and hollows in the ground, silent and cloaked in turf. Gainsthorpe in Lincolnshire is again a series of grassy dunes representing trackways, houses and dovecotes, illustrating lives moved on. And there are many more.[1]

Enclosure dramatically reshaped the countryside, changing and restricting people's movements. It reminds

---

* It should be noted that enclosure was a complex process that varied greatly from region to region. It was not a single 'thing'. It was also the result of a set of complex processes within society and the economy of the time.

us that mobility isn't always a freedom. The perambulating philosophers and rambling writers we met earlier all enjoyed freedom to move at will, as did the Roman elite and the boulevardiers of nineteenth-century Paris. They were privileged, or at least semi-privileged. But privilege and freedom are defined by their opposites, and never available to all.

In previous chapters we saw that movement has been defined by cultural norms, whether in John Travolta's twentieth-century Brooklyn or at Neolithic sites in Wiltshire. In this chapter we'll see that those cultures are themselves defined by freedoms and restrictions. Again, where archaeological evidence is not (yet?) available, we must look to the present and to the written historical record. And when we do, we see that as well as forcing people to move, the powerful also sometimes *restrict* movement. It can be used as both whip and chain.

As recently as 1967, the Criminal Law Act removed the offence of being a 'common night walker' from the English statute books. That offence had been created 700 years earlier, by Edward I in 1285. Known as the Statute of Winchester, it required every walled town and city to close at sundown, and put a curfew in place until sunrise, with watches in every settlement.

Anyone moving at night, known as common night walking, was likely to be a 'wastor' or thief, and detained by the night-watch. After all, if you were up and about at night you must be asleep during the day, and therefore idle and of no economic value.[2]

This legislation, extended in 1331 by Edward III, forcefully regulated people's ability to move around. Itinerants and vagrants could be harried at will. The Statute of Cambridge in 1388 introduced still more restrictions, prohibiting labourers and beggars from leaving the place they inhabited without 'reasonable cause' and a written testimonial – a sort of passport to be mobile. To move away from the land was to move away from the lord, and therefore their authority. The lord knew that to control movement was to control lives. As is still the case, geographic mobility is synonymous with social mobility.

At the same time, poverty throughout the medieval and early modern period caused many landless, place-less working-class people to be perpetually on the move, shifting groups of craftsmen, apprentices, pedlars and labourers engaged in a ceaseless search for work. 'A beggar lives here in this vale of sorrow,' wrote the poet and eccentric journeyman John Taylor* in 1621, 'and travels here today and there tomorrow, the next day being neither here nor there: but almost nowhere, and yet everywhere.'[3]

People who moved outside the cultural norm attracted suspicion, as they still do. Roma people, who originated in the Punjab, lived a largely nomadic lifestyle. Their itinerant life was seen as wild, an abomination to a civilised, settled society. In 1530 Henry VIII passed the Egyptians Act, which effectively legalised the brutal persecution of the 'outlandish people, calling themselves Egyptians'. This act was not repealed until 1856, but hostility towards 'Gypsies' persists (the word derives from the erroneous

---

* 'Eccentric' because, among other mad journeys, he once tried to sail from London to Queenborough in Kent in a paper boat.

name 'Egyptians'). Like roaming hunter-gatherers, Traveller groups are both romanticised and demonised.

*

Another period of enclosure, known as Parliamentary Enclosure, took place more recently, peaking twice. First, in the middle of the eighteenth century, then during the Napoleonic Wars in the early nineteenth century when the price of corn skyrocketed. Landowners petitioned Parliament to bring commons that had survived earlier enclosure – or 'wastes' as they were sometimes known – into private control, thereby substantially increasing the productivity and value of the land.

These areas, not wasteland at all but often rich in resources, such as heaths, moors, fells, fens, woodlands, rough pastures and boggy and scrubby land, lay outside arable fields. Although they were never in public owner-ship – these lands were private property – local commoners had long enjoyed certain permissive rights to use them, and often relied on them for their food and for their livelihoods.

These uses varied from place to place and over time, according to local customs, but usually included the right to pasture animals and collect fuel, such as wood, peat or coal; or perhaps furze (gorse), tods (bushy bundles of ivy and other foliage) or hassock (clumps of grass from wet and waterlogged ground). Commoners might collect herbs for culinary or medicinal use – foxglove, St John's wort or feverfew – or to make dyes. These might be for their own use or to be sold in markets.

Use of commons underpinned the economy of many rural parishes, and allowed people living near them to be independent and develop their own crafts and small-scale family industries. These included charcoal-burners, crook-makers, peg-makers, spindlers, chair bodgers, cottagers, woodmen, quarrymen, brickmen, potters and squatters. Of the latter, there was a general belief – more of a folk custom really – that if you could build a house overnight and have smoke rising from the chimney by morning you were entitled to possession of it and could remain on the land. In this way, many a night house, clod house or clay house formed part of the makeup of common land. Common lands were also places where people could freely pass from one parish to the next, using the many footpaths that crossed them.[4]

When Parliamentary Enclosure was awarded to a waste, it was surveyed and radically redesigned so that the land became subdivided into separate private landholdings. These new fields were then used to grow crops (wheat and barley) or feed for livestock (clover and sainfoin, turnips and mangelwurzels). Records show that on the Yorkshire Wolds, for example, not far from the landscape of Wharram Percy, sainfoin was being grown on newly enclosed land by the 1730s, clover by the 1750s, and turnips by the 1760s.

Later on, many moors became shooting estates. The Kinder Enclosure Act of 1840, for example, saw 1,352 acres on Kinder Moor in the Peak District enclosed for the shooting of grouse. And records show that in 1898 people out picking bilberries on Broomhead Moor, also in the Peak District, were turned away by hostile gamekeepers after it had become a sporting estate. Similar stories can be found across England.

Where before were huge expanses of open space, used and useful to countless families, there were now linear boundaries and new, privately owned rectangular fields enclosed by fences and quickset hawthorn hedges (hence its alternative name: quickthorn). As the poet John Clare put it, describing the enclosure of the wild Northamptonshire landscape of his childhood: 'In little parcels little minds to please.'

Land previously open to all inhabitants was closed off; and long-standing obligations, privileges and rights to the land were abandoned.* At a stroke, a way of life on common land was extinguished, and many local crafts went with it. Commoners now had to sell their own labour in order to survive.[5]

To see these transformations in the English landscape, just look at a map of the countryside for the ruler-straight boundaries that smash across it. Or even better, go out and see where the ridge and furrow of the medieval common fields underlies later hedges and ditches.

Some 4.5 million acres of manorial waste in England was enclosed under Parliamentary Enclosure; 50,000 acres of waste disappeared in Northamptonshire alone.[6] Parliamentary Enclosure saw moors drained, rivers straightened, old roads closed and new, straight ones built. Hedges, ditches, fences, pales and walls were put in to mark new boundaries shutting out the masses. Centuries-old public footpaths were abolished. This process added several miles

....

* As noted above for earlier enclosure, Parliamentary Enclosure was a complex process and for many at the time it was seen as 'improvement' to an irregular system that was no longer fit for purpose.

onto daily journeys, and tightly controlled the movements of the people using them. Writing in the nineteenth century, the polymath and poet William Barnes described this, using Dorset dialect, in his poem 'The Common a-Took In':

> Girt banks do shut up ev'ry drong [a narrow lane],
> An' scratch wi' thorny backs along
> Where we did use to run among
> The vuzzen [furze] an' the broom.

Alongside this, the mansions and newly planned landscapes of the gentry similarly closed the countryside, walling off land and footpaths and creating new, often private, straight roads and avenues of trees. 'The ten miles from Guildford to Leatherhead make one continued line of gentlemen's houses ... their parks or gardens almost touching one another,' wrote Daniel Defoe in 1722, in his *A Tour Through the Whole Island of Great Britain*.

Of course, we can find evidence of exclusion and restriction in other, older, boundaries visible in the archaeological record: Hadrian's Wall, for example, or the linear earthworks known as dykes dating from prehistory through to the medieval period, in British upland areas. These long ditches and earthen banks sometimes extend across kilometres of countryside. The early medieval linear earthworks of Offa's Dyke and Wat's Dyke along the English–Welsh border created visually powerful statements on the landscape symbolising – and actually determining – who belonged on either side.

Something similar can be seen later in the 1,000-mile-long, dense and thorny hedge that was planted by the

British to extend half the length of India, the archaeological remains of which are still visible in places. This
was designed to control the passage of salt, a valuable
source of tax income, by channelling travellers through
controlled gateways. The hedge formed a monstrous
obstacle to the movement of people living around it,
requiring large detours to get through, and impeding
their everyday movement.[7] Later still, there was the Berlin
Wall, traversable only at Checkpoint Charlie.

*

But where there's restriction, there's resistance. Mobility
can be a form of fight.

Again, we rely on the written record and our own
modern lives to see that. From the sixteenth century
onwards, many people expressed opposition to the enclosure of fields and common land through rioting, sedition
and protest. From this time, we also see an explosion
in the number of pamphlets expressing strong opinions
on enclosure. The term 'Leveller' was used to describe
people who protested by levelling the hedges, ditches
and fences that enforced enclosure. Kett's rebellion saw
16,000 people storm Norwich in 1549 in protest at
enclosure. In the seventeenth century there were riots at
Selwood in Wiltshire, Gillingham in Dorset, Feckenham
in Worcestershire, and many other areas. In the three
years between 1830 and 1833, there were thirteen riots
and acts of arson in Cambridgeshire alone.[8]

Participants were known as a 'mob' by landowners –
an abbreviation of the Latin *mobile vulgus*, 'moveable and
excitable common people'. And from this we get: the mob,

mobster, mob-handed and mob-rule. Another disapproving word, forged in the fire of movement, is trespass. This comes from the Old French *trespasser*, 'to pass across'.

William Wordsworth, who walked compulsively, observed enclosure as it happened around him:

> Whereso'er the traveller turns his steps,
> He sees the barren wilderness erased,
> Or disappearing.

Upheaval wasn't restricted to the countryside. Urban settings also saw resistance in the form of movement. The German philosopher Walter Benjamin wrote about the figure of the *flâneur* in his reflections on Paris in the first half of the twentieth century. *Flânerie* was the art of strolling or sauntering around the urban landscape and observing the hustle and bustle without being caught up in it. A little later, Guy Debord and Michel de Certeau prescribed the *dérive* as a revolutionary subversion of consumerism: creating new paths through the city by chance. Also *détournement*, in which spaces in the built environment are hijacked for alternative uses – much like skateboarding or parkour in our own times. Moving around in this detached way was seen as a form of resistance that discovered alternative, perhaps even suppressed, stories. Taken up by groups of radical poets and artists, it became a critique of post-war urbanism and capitalism. The underlying motive would be familiar to the Levellers: a sense of anger and loss as Paris was rebuilt from the 1950s to the 1970s, and the inner-city working-class population was uprooted and shunted out to housing blocks in the suburbs.

The more recent practice of psychogeography – drifting around urban environments and finding new stories to tell about it, as a micro-political act – is in the same tradition. By getting lost and making the familiar strange, parts of everyday life not typically paid attention to are opened up. Psychogeographic enquiry, and modern urban walker writers generally, use the *dérive* to map the way cityscapes and topography combine to create distinctive moods and spirits. Nostalgia and loss often play an important part in this, seen in the writings of Will Self, Ian Sinclair and Nick Papadimitriou, among others.[9]

Urban archaeology, which peers under the concrete of modern conurbations or lifts the rubble of brownfield sites, always felt similar to me; a form of psychogeography. I worked in that world in the early years of my career, as I mentioned. Excavating through modern rubble to soils from earlier times provided a sense of nostalgia and loss: it felt as if we were digging our way out of the modern metropolis to a pastoral past. In this environment, working in archaeology felt like a political act. Not everyone was happy to have us on site, arguing that we got in the way, delaying the march of progress. We rarely did slow things down, but we were somewhat apart from everyone else, fitting in with neither the other workers on the ground nor the besuited managers in their on-site offices. I always felt I was in someone else's world when I was on site, but never really knew whose world it was. And I positively embraced that sense of being an outsider. At the day's end, I'd join the masses pouring out of the surrounding office blocks and funnel into the nearest station to squeeze onto the London Underground. I took pleasure in this daily rhythm, especially the looks I received, sitting among the office suits in my frayed and mud-splattered T-shirt and multi-pocketed combat trousers (all the better for holding various-sized trowels, small brushes and little sealable finds bags). Typically, I'd read some worthy book: Darwin's *On the Origin of Species* perhaps, or Nietzsche's *Thus Spoke Zarathustra*. My own micro-political act.

Back in India, the lawyer and activist Mahatma Gandhi used walking as a kind of peaceful rebellion throughout his life. He travelled the length and breadth of the country campaigning, promoting, teaching and preaching. In 1930, he undertook an epic journey to the sea, to gather salt in breach of the manifestly unjust British salt tax. Hundreds of thousands of people were inspired to join him, resisting control through walking.

A couple of years later, a mass trespass took place at Kinder Scout in the English Peak District. This moorland had for generations been common land, but nineteenth-century Parliamentary Enclosure had seen it privatised and closed off. In 1932, after many small acts of trespass, 400–500 people came together at Kinder Scout to skirmish with gamekeepers and landowners over these access rights.[10] Not all rambling groups agreed with this approach, preferring to seek reform through parliamentary legislation, but the Mass Trespass was the beginning that ultimately led to both the formation of National Parks in the UK and the Right to Roam legislation in 2000, which changed the way people are able to move around the rural landscape. But pre-enclosure freedoms have not been recovered, and 'Trespassers Will Be Prosecuted' signs (entirely meaningless words since, for now at least, you cannot be prosecuted for trespass) remain a common sight.

Gandhi's Salt March and the Mass Trespass at Kinder Scout show that there's something primal about mass movement. When feelings are high, people all over the world take to the streets, sometimes in their millions. As you know if you've ever seen it up close, there is brute power in walking together. It is no coincidence, surely, that people working together to advance a shared cause are known as a 'movement'.

The barricade is a form of resistance too, and wilful immobility can be surprisingly effective. This was deployed to great effect by the 'Occupy' movement starting in 2011, which involved camping out, sometimes for weeks at a time, in financial districts, along certain streets, and within key buildings, to protest against social and economic inequalities, as well as corporate corruption. Perhaps they were inspired by African-Americans 'sitting in' at segregated 'whites only' restaurants in the struggle for civil rights during the 1960s, just as those African-Americans were inspired by others, reaching back throughout written history and beyond.

The powerful seek to restrict movement or compel it; so resistance takes the form of either motion or stillness. This takes us back to those few pieces of later pottery and the jettons at Wharram Percy. Is this evidence of unrecorded squatters surrounded by deserted buildings and clinging on to life in the village in the decades after abandonment? A family, perhaps, who refused to move on? After all, inaction can be action.

8. ROUTEFINDING: FOLLOWING THE OLD WAYS

....

In which we lose one prehistoric routeway,
but find two more

....

Walking along ridgeways became hugely popular in Britain in the nineteenth century. They run along hilltops, making use of the naturally hard surface. Many a national trail now follows a ridgeway.

They have frequently been declared prehistoric in origin. In 1893 the writer Kenneth Grahame declared that the ridgeway that runs through Wiltshire and Oxfordshire evolved from 'the primitive prehistoric track'. The Icknield Way, from eastern to southern England, was similarly described as a prehistoric route by several writers: Hilaire Belloc (in 1904), Hippisley Cox (1914) and Edward Thomas (1916). In 1933 the English historian George Beardoe Grundy described ridgeways generally as having 'a continuous existence going back into times long before history began'. In 1988 the journalist Richard Ingrams wrote a book with the title *The Ridgeway: Europe's Oldest Road*. More recently, in *The Old Ways*, Robert Macfarlane set off along the Icknield Way and the Ridgeway wishing them to be prehistoric routes.

I'm sorry to say that there's little evidence for them being prehistoric. Quite the opposite.

This erroneous assumption arose from the nineteenth-century belief that prehistoric people lived mainly on high ground, where their settlements, fields and monuments remained clearly obvious to the observer as upstanding earthworks. Prehistoric lives were less evident in the valleys and lowlands, and so it was guessed that these areas must have been uninhabitable, probably due – it was thought – to heavy clay, marshland and thick and impassable wildwood. It stood to reason that routes between settlements would be along ridges.

The guess is reasonable, but wrong. It is a visibility issue: archaeology is better preserved in these upland, but more historically peripheral, areas, and generally easier to see. Valleys, being more fertile, have been farmed and ploughed for millennia, erasing earthworks, while deposits have built up, sealing and concealing sites. With the development of landscape-wide archaeological prospection and remote sensing techniques such as aerial photography and geophysics, and vastly more archaeological excavations, we can see that the lowland areas were intensively lived in throughout prehistory. Much more so, in fact, than the upland areas, which begin to lose some of their importance in this light. And in fact, routes such as the Icknield Way could never have functioned as a long-distance path in prehistory since a number of long, linear prehistoric ditches and banks, evidence for ancient field boundaries, slash perpendicularly across the suggested route, showing no regard for it whatsoever, and these would have blocked passage.

Some ridgeways may date to the early medieval period – but not earlier. That goes for the Pilgrims' Way in Kent, the North Downs Way, the South Downs Way and the Jurassic Way, a limestone ridge that stretches across England from Banbury in Oxfordshire through to Lincolnshire.[1]

Evidence for prehistoric paths that can be found in the archaeological record, though often difficult to identify, includes parallel ditches, or double ridges, formed by ploughing and known as lynchets. Running between ancient fields, these show up best in aerial photographs.

Frequently used paths are easier to find because they erode the ground and create a scar, particularly where they descend a slope. When deeply incised they become sunken ways or holloways, as we saw in the first chapter, carved into existence through the erosive effects of travel by generations of people, animals, wheeled vehicles and rainwater pouring down them so that at times they become temporary riverbeds.

Over centuries of use, holloways can deepen by as much as six metres. They are timeworn manifestations of human travel. Literally hollowed out. And because of this scouring process they were previously thought to be undatable.

The snail man disagreed. Archaeologist Martin Bell has studied ancient snails for most of his life. Like me, he is passionate about paths and walking. He was responsible for the excavation of the Mesolithic footprints we have already seen in the Severn Estuary. Working on an archaeological site in Kent a few years ago, one of those fortuitous things happened to Martin that led to unexpected advancements in knowledge. The side of a nearby holloway collapsed, revealing deposits that had built up alongside it. These, he surmised, must be part of the lynchet – the ridge formed by ploughing – that once ran alongside the original routeway. They would date to the time the path had first formed, and were likely to contain ancient snail remains. By dating these deposits, he could establish the age of the start of the holloway.

Martin took soil samples and sieved them for any evidence.

Fortunately, snails were plentiful, and they told a story of a dramatically changing local environment. Originally wooded (suiting shade-loving woodland snails), it became open grassland, then came a covering of trees along the, by now, well-established routeway. Interestingly, later deposits included snails that were only introduced at the end of the Roman period, suggesting that the earlier deposits had formed before that – in prehistory.

Additional dating techniques confirmed this: uranium series dating of the snail shells uses the radioactive decay of uranium to calculate age, and optically stimulated luminescence (OSL) works by establishing when tiny grains of quartz in the soil were last exposed to sunlight. These showed that the early woodland phase was likely cleared, and the routeway established, in the Late Bronze Age or Early Iron Age, around 1000 BCE. This was further confirmed by pieces of prehistoric pottery from within these soils. Flanking deposits continued to build up through the Roman and medieval periods. As the routeway continued to be used, the path slowly eroded down, so that a shady, wooded bank along the holloway came into existence as early as 800 CE.

This story shows that with careful investigation and scientific analysis, and a can-do spirit, holloways can be dated. This holloway in Kent is at least 3,000 years old, and has been used continuously over that time.[2] I can't think of any other single feature, anywhere in the world, that was created so long ago and that is still used, and has been continuously, for the same purpose it was made for. It is astonishing. Think about that, next time you find yourself inside a holloway.

To me, they create the feeling that I've slipped through a crack in time. Holloways are not designed, constructed or part of a grand network. They represent 'desire lines' used for the everyday; paths that emerge as shortcuts between two points.

Entering a holloway can feel like disappearing into a magical landscape of its own, particularly one so deep that it is in semi-permanent shade and hidden from the surrounding countryside. I've sought solace in holloways on more than one occasion. Taking the shape of a tunnel – more so if there are trees from grown-out hedgerows arching overhead – they focus attention only on the light ahead, creating an unbeatable visual metaphor for life's journey, and the passing of deep time.

And they function as miniature nature reserves, providing shelter to bankside plants in winter and cool, dappled shade in summer.

*

But holloways are not the oldest paths we know about. Archaeologists have found Neolithic paths that remain preserved, believe it or not, despite being made of wood.

Many of these prehistoric timber trackways have been recorded in Europe's wet peatlands, including the Somerset Levels. The greatest numbers are in Ireland. Neolithic to Iron Age in date, these wooden walkways crossed boggy, sodden landscapes so that people could move around areas that were otherwise inaccessible. It's precisely because of the watery nature of the landscape that the timbers have been preserved, and we can clearly see the construction methods that were used. Amazingly, we can even identify the exact year the trees were felled by examining the patterns of annual growth rings in wood.

Peat is made of compressed fibrous layers of partially decayed plants in waterlogged environments. Their wet and either very acidic or very alkaline nature means that little rots away and so, each year, as the plants on the surface of the bog die off, they simply add another layer to the peat preserved beneath. Through this yearly process the bog slowly grows higher, sometimes reaching many metres above surrounding drier land. Although bone can dissolve away in this environment, other organic matter such as wood and cloth, or skin and hair, can be preserved as if in a pickling jar.

Some of the prehistoric peatland paths are simple: little more than lines of brushwood pegged in place. Others are more complex. The best known, and one of the earliest, is the exquisitely named Sweet Track near Glastonbury in Somerset, built across the otherwise impassable Avalon Marshes. Discovered in 1970 during peat extraction, it is named after its finder Ray Sweet. The science of dendrochronology tells us it was constructed between 3807 and 3806 BCE. The builders drove sharpened wooden poles obliquely into wet ground to form a V-shaped frame; then laid oak planks into this, and secured the planks with pegs to create a raised walkway. It was narrow, and would have only allowed for people walking along it in single file. It was maintained for a number of years before the growing peat swallowed it up.[3]

How were these trackways used? Probably as everyday local routes across permanently or seasonally water-logged ground; or to give access from dry land across marshland to channels of open water where canoes may have been moored. Either way, they provided conven-ient access to the rich resources of wetland areas, and we can easily imagine that hunting hides or similar existed at the end of some wooden paths. They also connected settlements. Remarkable evidence of prehistoric houses, preserved in peat, at Glastonbury and at Must Farm near Peterborough in the East Anglian Fens, prove that com-munities lived over watery areas in prehistory, making a mockery of the nineteenth- and early twentieth-century assumption that prehistoric folk feared the marsh. These prehistoric houses, just like the wooden trackways, have preserved a level of detail not normally seen from the archaeological record, which includes the wooden build-ings themselves.

The houses at Must Farm in the Cambridgeshire Fens date from around 1100 to 800 BCE, and are made up of at least four roundhouses built on stilts above a broad but shallow and slow-moving river. Each was connected to another by a raised walkway, and they were all encir-cled by a protective fence. Not long after the roundhouses were constructed, maybe only a year later, the buildings were consumed in a catastrophic fire that burnt the stilts, and the whole lot collapsed into the waters below. There they were so well preserved that archaeologists in 2015 and 2016 uncovered, three metres below the modern ground, not just the buildings, but people's belongings inside them, from the charred remains of furniture, to fine textiles and bundles of plant fibre ready to be made into yarn, and bobbins of thread about to be woven into cloth, the loom weights and spindle whorls ready nearby. There were wooden buckets and bronze weapons and tools, some with wooden handles, and little personal items including a razor blade and amber and glass necklace beads. There was even a splendidly made wooden box, small and delicate, but empty when found, so we don't know what was once kept in it. Something personal and precious, no doubt, that may have been salvaged in haste when the fire broke out. Stacks of burnished pots and wooden platters and bowls sat awaiting a dinnertime that never came, although some did contain meals that were being made, or eaten, when the fire started and householders ran for their lives. The food was a sort of pottage made from wheat and barley and herbs. This wasn't a settlement that had grown old and been abandoned, but one still in its first flush of youth; a thriving community. The archaeology here gives us an extraordinary, vivid glimpse of the flows of wetland life in the Late Bronze Age.[4]

Not all wetlands were lived in, and they can sometimes be charged with a powerful air of mystery. Neither land nor water, yet both at the same time, they were traditionally where boggarts lived and strange Jack-o'-lantern lights could sometimes be glimpsed. Water nymphs and bog sprites might lure the unsuspecting traveller. And wooden trackways led people deep inside them.

Many of the excavated wooden trackways seem to have been abandoned or swallowed up soon after construction. It has been suggested that some were specially built to get out into the sodden landscape for ceremonial purposes. The evidence? Archaeologists sometimes find artefacts that appear to have been placed in wetland areas deliberately. A polished green jade axe-head, soap-like to touch, was found in the spongy peat alongside the Sweet Track. This recalls the great number of stone axe-heads found deposited in rivers in the Mesolithic and Neolithic periods, or the many hoards of Bronze Age weapons in similar locations. Gifts to the water gods? To small-scale societies for whom taking from the landscape required something to be given back, a deposition like this made sense.

These riddling, liquid landscapes also preserve bog bodies: human remains, naturally mummified in the peat bog. Skin and hair, clothes and shoes – often turned black in the peat – are preserved in shocking, delicate detail. Many of the later bog bodies are evidence of accidents; folk who never returned home after losing their way or straying from the path. Some, although it is rare, have been found with walking staffs, or clutching clumps of peat as if desperately trying to claw their way out. One poor child, at Ballygudden in Ireland, had a belt around their neck, which – as one interpretation sees it – was the panicked mother's attempt to lasso and pull them out. The rescue failed and the child died, as did the mother whose body was found in the bog next to them. These can be fickle, dangerous environments. Other bodies are clearly suicides, or victims of violence, and sometimes they are very recent.

But some bog bodies are ancient, 2,000 and more years old, and they show that in the Iron Age and early in the Roman period people were killed, possibly as part of a sacrifice: an offering, perhaps in the same way axe-heads were deposited, but more so; the ultimate gift when times were at their grimmest. These people were not necessarily on the margins of society – quite the opposite, some may have been leaders. They were often carefully prepared prior to their gory (or perhaps glory) end, and probably went along with it all knowingly. They were usually stripped, with hair trimmed or cut off altogether, and nails tidied, before being taken out into the bog for their sleep eternal.

We can see this with the 30-year-old Tollund Man, an almost perfectly preserved bog body from Denmark. He was found not far from the village of Tollund in 1950 by a family of peat cutters. He was lying on his right side, his head turned and his black-stained leathery skin stretched thin. His eyes and lips are gently closed as if asleep, but only just, so that it seems if you spoke in anything but a whisper his eyes might flick open. At some point between 405 and 380 BCE his hair was cut short and he was taken to the bog. He was stripped naked, but for a leather belt around his waist and a beautifully made sheepskin cap on his head; the soft wool on the inside for greater warmth and comfort, and the straps passing under his chin and fastened with a bow on the side. He was given a final meal of gruel, made from barley, oats, wild seeds and fish, possibly cooked in the bog water itself (we know this from close analysis of the contents of his stomach). He was then hanged until dead with a plaited leather cord before being placed in the bog, the leather thong still tied around his neck.[5]

Two years later, in 1952, another Danish bog body, also around 30 years old, was discovered by peat diggers, this time near the village of Grauballe. Grauballe Man lived sometime between 400 and 200 BCE and his smooth hands speak of an easy life with little in the way of hard labour. Again, prior to death his clothing was removed and his hair, beard and moustache neatly trimmed. He was given a meal of gruel made from cereals, wild seeds and pork. His throat was then cut, cleanly, from ear to ear, before he was placed into the bog for the next 2,000 years.

In Britain, Lindow Man (or Pete Marsh as he's popularly known – how wonderfully human it is to name the nameless!) is another possible human sacrifice. He was found in 1984 by a peat extraction machine in Lindow Moss in Cheshire, where a number of bog bodies, or bits of bodies, had been found previously. He was killed and buried in the bog some decades later than the Danish bog bodies we've just seen, between the first and second centuries of the Common Era. His teeth were in excellent condition and his nails neatly clipped; he appears to have led a privileged life. On the day of his death, he was stripped naked except for a fox-fur armband; perhaps an amulet. His last meal was of barley, probably in the form of a griddle cake, as well as some meat. When death came it was sudden and thunderously brutal. He was hit hard on the back, forcing him to his knees, and then struck twice on the back of the head, first with a blunt axe and then with a cudgel. Still alive, but perhaps unconscious, he was garrotted with a length of animal sinew, his throat was cut and he was stabbed in the chest. Finally, his neck was broken. Murdered in multiple ways, his death was a ritualised performance. Thinking about the narrowness of the wooden trackways, we see that it would have been difficult to carry him out to the bog. Did he walk to his own doom?

PART 3

Trailing

9. FEET FOLLOW HOOVES: WALKING WITH ANIMALS

....

*In which we see the special importance of
the dog and the horse*

....

I heard a story a while ago that goes something like this: when Welsh drovers took their animals on the hoof from Wales to the markets in London, a journey of several weeks, they brought their dogs to keep the animals moving and in check.

They followed the same route and stayed at the same wayside inns each time. Every night the drovers would install the animals on nearby pastureland, and in the morning they would pay the innkeeper just a little more than needed, each time.

Eventually, they would arrive at the market and sell the animals, then stay on in London, either to make a little more money helping with the autumn harvests, or to enjoy spending some of the money they had just made in the city taverns. Or perhaps a bit of both. No longer needing their trusty hounds, they would turn them loose. After years of doing this trip, older dogs showed young ones the way. Retracing their steps, the dogs would arrive at the inns where they had stayed previously. The inn-keeper would give them food, water and shelter. And in this way the dogs made their own way back home.*

It's a wonderful story that has stayed with me, and there are many others like it to be heard up and down the country, capturing and celebrating the complex relationship between humans and animals, moving around together and separately.[1]

At the risk of stating the obvious: dogs do many things for us that we prefer not to do, and some things that we can't do.

They herd sheep, drive cattle, and retrieve things like downed waterfowl without ripping them to pieces. They guard our homes, protecting people and live-stock from predators. They lead the blind and guide the hearing-impaired. They use their scenting ability to track hunted animals and to find people who are lost. Working with the military and the police, dogs can sniff out drugs, guns, explosives and escaped convicts. They

---

* This story was told to me by my late father-in-law, Chris Sayer, who was a superior raconteur and much missed.

can be used as beasts of burden, pulling sledges in snowy landscapes. The Pawnee people in North America used dogs to haul supplies, such as tent poles or firewood, either by dragging them on a wooden frame known as a travois, or in saddle bags known as 'dog sacks'.[2]

For as long as there have been stories, there have been stories of dogs.

In Greek mythology, Sirius was sent to the heavens as a messenger and became the Dog Star – the star that shines brightest. In a thirteenth-century Welsh tale, Gelert the dog is left to look after prince Llywelyn the Great's baby son. Llywelyn returns from the hunt to find his child's cradle upturned and the muzzle of his hound Gelert covered in blood. In grief and anger Llywelyn plunges his sword into the dog's heart, only to find, in the next instant, his baby alive and unharmed beside the dead body of a wolf that Gelert had bravely fought off in his master's absence. The Scottish story of Greyfriars Bobby tells of a little terrier who kept his nightwatchman master company when he was on duty. Bobby, ever the faithful companion, never left his side, and even after his master died, he sat on his grave until his own death fourteen years later.

There are many other stories like this all over the world. How far back do they go?

Dogs were domesticated before any other species, and became key to everyday hunter-gatherer life. One archaeological site shows this particularly well.

In the southernmost part of Sweden there is a small village on a stunning white sandy beach. The village is Skateholm. Inland of the beach and just north of

Skateholm are wetlands that were once part of a large prehistoric lagoon. Realising that the area would have been rich in resources in the Mesolithic period, a team of archaeologists in the 1980s, led by the late Lars Larsson – a titan of the discipline – set out to excavate what would have been a small island. Their work was well rewarded. They uncovered a series of 7,000-year-old Mesolithic hunter-gatherer settlements, and found the inhabitants buried across two cemeteries.

Mesolithic burials are extraordinarily rare. At Skateholm they recorded almost a hundred. Careful excavation clearly showed that complex burial rites had taken place. These involved the delicate placing of grave goods, such as stone knives, antlers, axes and ornaments, such as animal teeth that would have decorated belts. Choice animal parts were placed next to the body, presumably as food to be eaten on the journey to the afterlife. Food was evidently consumed by spectators too, for their leftovers were incorporated into the backfill of the graves. Parts of the deceased's bodies were covered in red ochre, a powder made from grinding iron-rich stone. The symbolism of this we can only guess at, but perhaps it represented blood.

What is particularly fascinating is that among the human burials are a dozen or so dog graves, and a number of these dogs had burial gifts too. One was buried with a decorated antler tool and three flint knife blades. Five were sprinkled with red ochre in the same manner as the human burials.[3] Clearly, the dogs were recognised as companions, even at this early point of dog domestication – perhaps even considered a part of the family, in death as in life.

I don't think that this is difficult to understand. I have had dogs all my life – the current incumbent being Bard, a Bedlington Whippet so scruffy that one passing stranger referred to him as 'raggedy-arsed', a good description. This raggedy-arsed dog, like the others I've had, found a way into the heart of our family. As a puppy he won our hearts when he played, and pounced, and chewed, and licked, and then looked up with huge, pleading brown eyes. And as he grew up, he has become warm and intelligent, and still cuddles up on the sofa, or – yes, I admit it – the bed. He has become one of the family. One of us.

We can't tell if the dogs buried at Skateholm were raggedy-arsed, but, while being careful about imposing modern views on the past, we can assume that there was a similar sense of connection. Dogs are nurtured in much the same way children are: guided and counselled to live correctly along a path to maturity. They never become fully human, but they understand certain aspects of human communication – 'dognition' as the ethologist Frans de Waal puts it.[4]

Encapsulated in the archaeological evidence from Skateholm, and in the drover story at the beginning of this chapter, is the complex 15,000-year relationship between humans and dogs – and other animals – and our movements together. They provide unconditional companionship, which helps our well-being; not least by getting us out of the house for exercise and contemplation. Did Mesolithic dog owners get pulled on a lead? Did their dogs force a slower pace while reconnoitring and retracing scents? Just like dogs today, they would have darted from side to side to check up on things, gather information, observe the tracks of other animals and sniff at scent marks, pausing to anoint trees and the prehistoric equivalent of lamp posts with their own scent in response.[5]

For humans and dogs alike, this experience of movement together has changed very little over thousands and thousands of years.

*

Tracking prey is another way in which human movement has been choreographed with animals. The prehistoric footprints we saw in earlier chapters, around the muddy margins of lakes and estuaries, often contain evidence of this. The footprints at Formby, for example, show human trails running parallel with large red deer prints; the humans slow, occasionally stopping and then carrying on, stalking perhaps. Successful stalking and tracking require a precise understanding of the sounds and smells of a variety of animals, and an ability to identify footprints, and even fragments of footprints, and other markers such as displaced leaves or twigs. Even a pebble out of place might indicate the direction of an animal's travel.

Like humans, animals make networks of paths, which the tracker needs to understand and mentally disentangle so that they can follow the right one. In tall grass, distinct paths may be discerned by strands bent in the line of travel. In dense bushes, branches might be pulled in a particular direction, or leaves turned upward or bruised, subtly changing their colour. A small gap in a hedge or bush might be an animal path; a smeuse, as it's known. In the morning, where there's dew, or after rain, any disturbance of otherwise uniform water droplets might be noticeable. And cobwebs may be broken as an animal moves through them.

The tracker needs to differentiate between tracks made in the last few hours and others made days ago. The age of the spoor helps the tracker determine whether they will be able to catch up with the animal. Are the droppings fresh and slimy or old and dry? Is there saliva still on the bushes? If near water, can you see splash marks?

And the tracker needs to understand an animal's behaviour to anticipate and predict its movements. If they understand its normal habitat, they might be able to ignore the tracks and head straight to, say, a watering place or a feeding ground.

This knowledge is gained through a lifetime of continuous learning, of watching and carefully observing animals and the tracks they make. Modern hunting societies, such as Kalahari hunters, tend to learn these things from a very young age, through play and storytelling and trying to track smaller creatures, carefully reconstructing their habits and movements, as well as watching adults and listening intently to their conversations. As adults, hunters spend hours discussing the habits and movements of different animals.

The trackers themselves need to move in particular ways to follow animals. This may involve moving at a brisk pace while scanning the ground ahead, taking care not to step on and spoil the track. Or staying well back so as not to scare the animal, but close enough to be able to catch it.

As they come closer to the animal, their movements will become slower, stealthier and more cautious. Kalahari hunters regularly gesture to one another through hand signals, indicating the direction and speed of movement, flicking fingers to indicate if the animal is nearby. They may use the cover of bushes, and go down on hands and knees. In long grass, they may lie on their stomachs and pull themselves along with their elbows.

They put themselves in the animal's position and think like it; feel like it. If domesticated dogs have (even slightly) 'become' like humans, so hunters must become like the animals they follow.[6] Their movements and perceptions of the world are determined as much by the feet of their quarry as by their own.

*

The same is true of pastoralists who spend much time walking with their animals. In order to be alert to the moods and motivations of sheep, a shepherd needs to see the world through sheep's eyes, to understand their rhythms of grazing.

The anthropologist Pernille Gooch describes the experience of goat herding in Sweden, and contrasts it with buffalo herding. As she describes it, with goats a successful herder must take command – essentially, become the she-goat and perceive the world as a she-goat. That way, when the herd becomes restless it is easy to lead them somewhere new. The goat herder leads from the front. Buffalo herding, by contrast, means walking behind: buffalo know their way from summer pasture along the annual migration route to winter grounds and will only go at their own speed. The successful buffalo herder follows. With goats, Gooch says, it's a case of 'feet-leading-hooves'. With buffalo, it's 'feet-following-hooves'.[7]

And because walking with different species of animal requires distinct styles of moving, it produces disparate perceptions of landscape, and leaves distinctly different traces.

Throughout written history – and probably earlier, in prehistory too – the British countryside thronged with herds and herders, relying on networks of droveways and tracks. By at least the seventeenth century, drovers were moving animals over huge distances, bringing cattle from Wales or the Highlands of Scotland to English pastures for fattening, before they were sold in the markets in the south and east of England.

Sheep were driven from places such as the Wiltshire Downs over the Ridgeway and Icknield Way to Thetford market in Norfolk. Flocks of turkeys were taken from Norfolk to Smithfield in London. Pigs, much harder to herd, were driven from Wales, Devon and Cornwall to Bristol, and sometimes further, to London. I honestly can't imagine what it must be like herding pigs for even a short journey, let alone a long one, but it must be pretty intense.

Geese were moved all over Britain, usually after harvest, to feed on the grain left among the stubble in fields on the way. The largest goose drove was from Lincolnshire and the Fens to the Michaelmas Goose Fair in Nottingham, and 'Stubble Goose' was a traditional dish for Michaelmas.

Animals were shod for these long journeys: cattle had metal shoes, pigs had woollen boots with leather soles on their trotters (and were often muzzled). Turkeys were also fitted with little leather boots. Geese, apparently harder to shoe, were driven through a tray of tar, mixed with sawdust and grit, to create a protective pad.[8]

Island cattle, needing to be brought to the mainland, were taken on boats if there were any. Otherwise, they were made to swim across. This happened across the Menai Strait in North Wales, until the Telford Bridge joined Anglesey to the Welsh mainland. In other places, they had to make hurried journeys across sands at low water.[9]

This is no romantic work, and must have been made up of long, exhausting, hunger-inducing days, moving in difficult conditions and bad weather with uncooperative animals. To help with these journeys, throughout the medieval and post-medieval periods, distinctive drove routes emerged – known as droveways, driftways or green roads – wide enough to accommodate the animals. At certain pinch points in the landscape these are made up of multiple parallel routes to prevent congestion and tailbacks, since they were generally being used at the same times each year. The archaeological remains are still visible in many places. Where there was no road or path, routes were marked out with Scots pines or, on the chalklands of southern England, with yew trees.[10]

Long-distance moving of animals like this requires watering, grazing and places where livestock could be shod, as well as accommodation for the drovers. Overnight lodging was normally at inns, usually with good pasture and a name such as The Drover's Arms, some of which still exist today. For the return journey, when animals were gone and purses were full, innkeepers would often lay on festivities, such as wrestling and boxing matches, a bit like the fairs we saw for pilgrims on holy days.

Grazing was provided by farmers renting fields en route for an overnight stay, or on village greens. Water was a key requirement, and cattle in particular needed a sizable water source such as a running stream. Blacksmiths prospered from the passing drover traffic, repairing cattle and horse shoes damaged on the journey. In this way, through their movements, drovers – like pilgrims before them – supported entire communities.[11] A droveway didn't just link places, it also created and sustained them.

That said, it must have been chaos each time drovers and their dogs and stock passed through a village, or flooded into market towns. A drover's life was obviously highly mobile, and from the mid-sixteenth century a licence was issued to distinguish them from beggars and the like. From the seventeenth century they had to carry a certificate of respectability, which required them to be over 30, a householder and a married man.[12]

Despite being thought of as wild and unkempt due to their high mobility, drovers earned a respectable wage compared to farm labourers and were highly trusted, which is not surprising as they often brought large sums of money back from the markets, needing to carry it past highwaymen and thieves. Court records show that drovers were occasionally robbed on the roads, though, or hoodwinked in the towns and cities, not least by prostitutes. Getting lost was also an ever-present threat. Given their position of trust and knowledge of the roads, drovers were frequently asked to carry important documents and letters to the towns. (After the Jacobite rising of 1745, drovers were the only civilians permitted to carry arms.[13]) And they carried news back with them, stories of events and changing fashions in the outside world, like prototype postal worker-journalists.

*

Like dogs, horses are naturally social creatures. And like dogs, horses have developed a close partnership with humans. This is why they are sometimes termed 'big dogs'. The introduction of horses to some groups appears to have led to a decrease in the importance of dogs; as happened with the previously mentioned Pawnee.[14]

Wild horses were present in the land that was to become the British Isles from about 17,000 years ago up until around 10,000 years ago. They were hunted and eaten, but not ridden. They became locally extinct for the next few thousand years, the result of changing environmental conditions as global temperatures continued to warm following the end of the last glacial period. I have heard people say that the ponies in the New Forest in southern England are survivors of the Ice Age and direct descendants of these wild horses, but this is not true. There is no good evidence for horses surviving into the later part of the Mesolithic or at any point in the Neolithic in Britain.

The horse was first domesticated in Kazakhstan around 5,500 years ago, where mares were corralled for meat and milk, and probably ridden occasionally too. But the ancestors of modern horses actually came from herders on the western Eurasian steppe, in what is now southern Russia, who domesticated wild horses around 4,200 years ago and then used them as mounts.[15] We will hear more of these steppe herders later in the book; they are rather important to our story.

We will never know what crazy daredevil first threw themselves on the back of a wild horse, but presumably it was somebody with a base-jumper's adrenaline-fuelled energy and willingness to bruise. Over the next few centuries, descendants of these Russian riders and their wonderful steeds galloped across Eurasia, changing cultures as they went. Some horses had arrived in Britain by the end of the Bronze Age, with many more throughout the Iron Age. All native British horse breeds developed from these, or from later introductions. What a vision they must have been!

This new form of movement changed everything, by extending the previous limits of human mobility and opening new opportunities to trade. Flows of people, goods and knowledge increased, as did the ability to herd other livestock further afield to new pastures. Riding on horseback provided a lofty position that enabled herders to control vastly greater numbers of animals more efficiently.

Horses were, from the beginning, admired in themselves: powerful, fast, brave and faithful, as well as highly sexed. They became mobile emblems of wealth and prestige. Ownership of horses, as well as knowledge of how to ride them, created an elite, literally raising the status of their owners above others. In this way, the arrival of the horse was transformative, not just for mobility, but for the way it created (or increased) social inequality and entrenched power.

People who do ride horses frequently comment on the sense of oneness they get with the animal, the shared fluidity of movements and the intense connection. We get a glimpse of this close relationship in the British Iron Age, from which time human and horse bones are sometimes found together in pits and in graves, as we'll see later. Horses are also key to the iconography of the time: on coins that depict human-headed horses, and in horse-shaped brooches.

The Uffington White Horse, a huge chalk figure carved onto the hillside of the Berkshire Downs in southern England, dates to the end of the Bronze and beginning of the Iron Age. This English equivalent of a Peruvian Nazca Line is the outline of a vast leaping horse, 110 metres long. Its original symbolism is lost to us, but it has been argued by Joshua Pollard – who we last saw re-analysing Woodhenge and The Sanctuary in Wiltshire – to represent the sun-horse. This feature of many Indo-European mythologies presents the divine sun as being pulled across the sky by a horse or horse-drawn chariot during the day, and transported through the underworld by boat or chariot at night. Below the Uffington White Horse is Dragon Hill, a huge Silbury-like mound protruding from the earth. It is argued that this was a representation of the sun being pulled behind the horse. People have often suggested that this, like Silbury, is an artificial mound. In a small but very interesting project I once drilled into it, to see what it was made of (I had all the relevant permissions, of course). Alas, it proved to be an entirely natural mound, made of solid chalk. But I think that the suggestion that it was thought of as the sun is a good one.[16]

Similar iconography appears in later prehistoric European rock art, as well as some marvellous metalwork figurines, such as the horse-drawn sun chariot from Trundholm Mose in Denmark. Dating to between 1400 and 1300 BCE and now in the National Museum of Denmark in Copenhagen, this elegant bronze artefact was ploughed up by a farmer trying to reclaim a bog in north-western Zealand in 1902. He thought at first it was a toy, and gave it to his daughter to play with, but its importance was eventually guessed at, and the National Museum came knocking. It comprises a cast bronze model of a horse pulling an upright disc, 25 centimetres in diameter. On one side of the disc is a thin sheet of highly decorated gold foil so that it glows like the sun, while the other is dulled and darkened. The disc sits on an axle attached to two spoked wheels, and the horse also stands on axles that are attached to four more spoked wheels. Everything about this 54-centimetre-long artefact speaks of movement. Pulled from east to west, we have the day with the sun burning gloriously; turn it around and the horse now pulls the moon in the other direction. Sun and moon; day and night. The horse's central role in keeping them ever moving is clear.

Throughout history, horses have been credited with supernatural powers and have become part of cosmologies. The human–horse hybrid is a common theme, such as the centaur of Greek mythology. And it is probably no coincidence that a wooden horse allowed the Greeks to take Troy.

Our relationship with animals generally is intimate, emotional and, more often than not, respectful. For much of the past we have lived in close quarters with animals and got to know their individual mannerisms, peccadilloes and lineages. They provide structure for our social and symbolic worlds. We've shared joy, grief and exhilaration together. We are inextricably joined, and that relationship has long conditioned human movements: the speed we move at, the routes we take, the trails we leave behind.[17] Some animals have caused human feet to fall into step with theirs, while others required large detours to avoid them – fields of bullocks or, in the past, wolves, bears and six-foot-at-the-shoulder aurochs.

10. TRANSHUMANCE:
TRAVERSING THE UPLANDS

In which we see that domesticating animals did not mean settling down

Unlike droving, an existential dead-end from which livestock never returned, some shared human–animal journeys of the past were round trips. An example of that is the seasonal movement in search of pasture.

This is known as transhumance, a word that in every way embodies movement. Derived from the Latin *trans* meaning 'across', and *humus*, 'ground', it describes the practice of moving farm animals on a seasonal cycle from their winter location to a summer one. This usually involves walking from fertile valleys where they spent the winter to higher summer pastures on moors, heaths, hills and mountains.

Moving between coastal saltmarsh and inland grassland is another form of transhumance. This occurred in south-east Wales, to and from the Fens in eastern England, and on the Somerset Levels in the west. Somerton, on the edge of the Levels, meant 'place used only in the summer'; a word that now lends its name to the whole county of Somerset.[1]

Transhumance allowed distant pastures to be exploited while leaving those nearer home to recuperate, as well as freeing them up to grow crops and hay, having been freshly manured.

I'm fascinated by transhumance. Not because I look back at it with a romantic nostalgia (or perhaps I do), but because, as I've remarked before, I'm drawn to the everyday, to things others think of as peripheral, but which were once of great importance to many people. It's so much more interesting and relevant to me than the goings-on of chieftains, royals or great leaders. Give me paths over the pyramids. Give me a good, deeply incised holloway over the finest buildings the world has to offer.

This type of movement has been practised around the world for thousands of years, and still is in some places, such as the Alps or the Scandinavian peninsula. Until recently it was very common in the British Isles in certain areas, continuing into the twentieth century in the western regions of Ireland, and even to just after the Second World War on the Isle of Lewis in Scotland. People moved with their animals, usually heading off in May, returning sometime in November; traditionally from Mayday (or Beltane) to Hallowe'en (Samhain, or All Saints' Day in the Christian calendar), although there was considerable variation to this. August was the height of the summering season for cattle in Britain.

Distances travelled varied but didn't need to be very far: the norm was somewhere between two and twelve kilometres from valley to pasture. In Mediterranean regions, where there are diverse climates, longer distances were common. The Mesta of medieval Spain is one such: tens of thousands of Merino sheep and their herders migrated between the northern and southern parts of the country.[2]

This occasionally happened in the British Isles too, and medieval England saw the transfer of sheep from different estates over large distances. Pigs were taken to wood pastures in the Weald of Kent and Sussex, travelling up to 30 or so kilometres, to feed on acorns and beech mast in the short autumn season that these are available.[3]

The threat of wolves, rustlers and other dangers, combined with the need to tend and regularly milk dairy cows and ewes, meant that people stayed with their animals on these pastures. It was often young women and girls, and sometimes boys too, that travelled with the beasts and lived on the summer pastures with them, milking them twice daily and churning it into butter.

Obviously, some form of accommodation was required, and a great variety of herders' houses were once visible across the British landscape. In the north of England and Scotland these were known as shielings, while the lowland winter settlements were wintersteads. In Wales the summer pasture was *hafod* and the winter sites *hendref*, while in Cornwall it was *havos* and *hendre*. In Ireland the herders stayed in booley huts, a word derived from the Irish *buaile*, meaning 'milking place in summer pasturage', and the practice was known as booleying.[4] Similar practices occurred in Sweden, Iceland and elsewhere.

Eighteenth- and nineteenth-century travellers to Scotland noted that people tending herds of milch cows stayed in beehive-shaped huts with walls made of earth sod and stone rubble. Some of these shielings still stand in the Scottish Highlands and islands. On Bodmin Moor in Cornwall they seem to have used similar corbelled beehive stone huts, although these are less well preserved. Some of the lumps and bumps still visible on Dartmoor are probably the earthwork remains of these buildings – few have even been recorded, let alone excavated. Excavated booley houses in Ireland indicate similar constructions, although they were adapted to specific places in the landscape. Some were rectangular, others oval, while some were completely irregular. They were made out of stone or sods of earth, or a combination of the two. Some even incorporated large boulders or natural outcrops in their walls. A bit like a small prehistoric roundhouse, these huts would have been enough for a bed, an open fire and some storage.[5]

Equivalent sites existed in lowland zones: the cabins and lodges of the 'lookers' of Romney Marsh in Kent, for example, or the 'denns' of the Weald, where swine and cattle were grazed.

For the young people, living away from home in remote landscapes must have been akin to entering another world; a state where different rules applied, and where individuals were outside the regular rhythms and routines that controlled normal life.

Homes were never too far away, of course, and regular contact would have been maintained every few days. But still, being away from parental control, youths could do what young people have always done. Or at least dreamed of doing. This is suggested in a mid-nineteenth-century account of transhumance in County Donegal in Ireland: while young women stayed in booleys, 'occasionally the young men came up from their neighbourhood far away, and they had a nice merry night, with their own music and dancing and fun.'[6] Perhaps this is what Julie Andrews meant when she sang that the hills are alive with the sound of music.

This form of transhumance clearly allowed young women and adolescent girls the opportunity to have a good time and enjoy themselves with boys, singing, dancing and playing games in the evenings. No doubt romantic encounters happened too, the hints of which can be found in contemporary folk songs, and in thirteenth- and fourteenth-century Icelandic sagas.

These sunlit uplands allowed a certain amount of freedom for teenagers, and must have been something of a rite of passage. It seems to me that life is poorer for the loss of this. A loss no doubt caused by the wider processes of enclosure. We shouldn't underestimate the importance of transhumance to social life, and the way it would have strengthened bonds between people that probably lasted a lifetime.[7]

These upland areas were liminal spaces, separate from everyday lives. As with the bogs we've seen previously, that liminality could easily become associated with supernatural events. Many a folk story is associated with shielings and booleys. In the Hebrides in Scotland the story of the *Shieling of the One Night* was often told or sung around a fire. This story changes depending on who is telling the tale, but it generally involves a being of some sort – a beast, a faerie, a kelpy or an old hag – tricking and murdering the shieling's occupants.

Similar stories of booley sites in Ireland tell of encounters with hags that can transform into hares and steal milk, or curse the people living in booley huts, and of strange and dangerous men who abduct young women and take them away as their brides.[8]

Clearly many of these stories are moral or practical warnings to the young: be on your guard and don't allow strangers into your huts. There's a tension in them between freedom and control; between the needs for young people to go away with the animals and be independent, and the natural desire of parents to protect and look after them.

Transhumance varied from region to region, and didn't always involve the young. In some places, Dartmoor, for example, a sort of professional herdsman developed in the medieval period. These men were paid to look after large collective herds on summer pastures on behalf of different landowners. Their job was mainly to prevent the animals from straying beyond the boundaries, but to care for them too.[9]

Being a herder in these far-off locations, whether girl or boy, young or old, was no pastoral idyll. They were expected to keep order in these remote areas, since noise and unrest would disturb the grazing livestock. Cattle rustling was an ever-present threat, as were wolves. None could perform their duties without a degree of grit and stamina.

*

As impermanent, occasional forms of movement, both droving and transhumance played a big part in the social life of pastoral societies. They would have led to distinct ways of seeing and understanding the landscape. People from different sections of society mingled together, exchanging information and news of distant events, as well as physical objects. Ideas surrounding status and wealth more broadly could be explored while moving animals, and the quality of the flock or herd – the visual expression of both status and wealth – could be inspected. And the distinctive rhythms of their mobility would have provided those involved with an exclusive identity.

Seasonal transhumance and droving broadened the social realm. They left their mark on the countryside too, from place-names – such as the suburb of Swansea in South Wales known as Hafod, or Buaile h'Anraoi in North Mayo, Ireland; there's also a Shiel Burn in Moray, Scotland, and a Somersbury Wood (and its counterpoint Winterfold Heath) in leafy Surrey in England – to the earthworks of herder huts, to deeply etched lines flowing from downland into valleys. Along these dense networks of lanes and tracks animals and humans flowed together.

Many of these paths and tracks are indicated now by a lace of banks and ditches that have enclosed and subdivided Britain for 4,000 years. Fields from as early as the Bronze and Iron Ages, incorporating networks of these lanes between them, can be found all over the chalk downland of Wessex, on Dartmoor, in the Thames Valley and across southern Britain, as well as on the edge of the Fens, and from Nottinghamshire to Yorkshire.[10]

Trackways through enclosed fields enabled animals to be driven through areas of arable without fear of damage to the crops. They were routes that developed as much from the form and folds of the landscape as the behaviour of the animals themselves. Within these small enclosed fields and along the integrated tracks, the lives and livelihoods of countless people have played out over millennia. By repeated ploughing, growing crops and herding animals, they have been etched into the landscape.

And many early routeways survive as tracks and public footpaths. I walk along an old droveway with Bard as part of our daily outings. While these tracks are now quiet lanes, they would once have thronged with great varieties of beasts grunting and bellowing, lowing and bleating. To this we can add the blowing of horns and the shouting of herders, the galloping of hooves, and barking of dogs. To say nothing of the muck and mud trampled and hoof-churned into a pismire. It must have been quite a spectacle; a great stinking caravan of people and animals blocking the road. Droveways were noisy, dirty affairs, but the lanes themselves imposed some order on these scenes.

11. WANDERLAND: SHAPING
AND BEING SHAPED

*In which a change of path and scenery leads
to alternative ways of walking*

Roads are sometimes flat and even, sometimes bumpy. And sometimes a road that was smooth becomes rutted without you really knowing exactly at what point that change happened.

The professional road I was on had taken me from working in development-led archaeology, to English Heritage, to teaching at university. It had been rich, varied and joyful. But at some point, as I was teaching – as I was writing the early chapters of this book in fact – it became uncomfortable.

If I had wheels, they'd have come off.

Falling student numbers, senior management concerns, and a review of the department. Like others, I found myself sitting in front of panels of people I had never met before, being asked questions about my value to the university. In my beaten state, each question diminished me, lessened my own worth, and I became helplessly wretched.

Over these weeks, my Chilterns walk was a solace. I stamped out my seething anger along the woodland path, and imagined biblically bad things on my interrogators. But generally, by about halfway through the journey, the tangled woodland landscape and the friendly familiarity of the path soothed my soul. Peace, of a sort, would settle over my frayed mind. *Solvitur ambulando*; it is solved by walking.

As well as getting bumpy, roads can unexpectedly change direction. Just as my own path started to look like a dead-end, an alternative course appeared ahead of me in the form of a job offer to teach at the University of York. Of course, I accepted. My family packed our lives into boxes, and, like generations before us, we moved.

I'm writing this on the edge of the North York Moors. A glorious landscape, rich and fresh. In places, it is still wonderfully wild, although decades of mismanagement from shooting estates – created by Parliamentary Enclosure – has left its scalp scorched and abused. It is full of paths, and many deeply incised holloways that once were well-used droveways and transhumance tracks.

Often, the stress of a situation doesn't fully manifest itself until after the danger has gone, and so it was with me. After a year of tumult, exhausted, it all hit me. My mind and body crumbled and then broke apart, so that I felt the atoms that made me had disintegrated and drifted away.

Once again, I found relief in paths, which provided me with refuge and direction. Especially the holloways, whose steep sides felt like they embraced and protected me from the outside world. I was particularly drawn to the darker and more tangled holloways; the ones rarely walked nowadays. In those early days after the move, I would sit in them, hidden from all human life, and weep. In my self-pity, I imagined melting into the ground and becoming mud; like an old cob wall re-joining the soil it had been made from. But slowly, through walking and the love of people around me, I got better.

The path I had walked in the Chilterns is now in my past. I look forward, with new paths to tread, new woodlands to explore.

I mention these details not because they make me unique but for the opposite reason: they are, I imagine, familiar to anyone who has uprooted, dislocated themselves. There is excitement and opportunity, but behind and beneath that there may be sadness and pain.

*

In 1921, a farmer outside Egtved in Denmark discovered what turned out to be a Bronze Age burial site.

Excavators found the remains of a girl aged between sixteen and eighteen. She died around the year 1370 BCE. In a reversal of the usual state of archaeological preservation, her skeleton had largely decayed away, with just 29 of her teeth surviving, but – incredible as it sounds – her blonde shoulder-length hair and neatly trimmed fingernails had been preserved, as well as a small amount of brain tissue, in the oxygen-free atmosphere under her burial mound. Traces of her skin could be seen at first too, although that disintegrated soon after her discovery.

Her clothing had also survived amazingly well, so we can see that she had been dressed in a short, tailored wool blouse with elbow-length sleeves, a woollen sash with an attached belt-plate wrapped around her exposed midriff, and around her hips was a knee-length skirt, formed of hanging lengths of cord. On her feet were foot wraps and leather shoes. Around each arm was a bronze ring, and in one ear an earring.

This teenage girl was buried on an ox hide inside an oak-log coffin, and with her she had a comb made of horn, a birch-bark box and a bark vessel containing the residue of beer sweetened with honey. Inside the box was a bronze awl and a hair net. Poignantly, a small bundle of cloth at her feet contained the cremated remains of a younger child. Placed on the edge of the coffin was a little yarrow flower, a final goodbye present from her mourning family, perhaps; a present that tells us the burial took place in summer.

Now known as the Egtved Girl, she has since inspired books, a film and even a musical reimagining her life. But the reason I mention her here is that she had not been born in southern Scandinavia at all.

Chemical analysis of her teeth demonstrated that she moved there as a child, while additional analysis of chemical isotopes in her hair and fingernails show that for at least the last two or so years of her life she had travelled backwards and forwards a number of times from southern Scandinavia to somewhere else, possibly south-eastern Sweden or Rogaland in Norway.

In 1935, another burial site was discovered in Denmark. This one contained the remains of a seventeen- or eighteen-year-old girl from Jutland. Now known as the Skrydstrup Woman, she too was buried in an oak-coffin grave under a mound, and at approximately the same time as the Egtved Girl – in this case, 1300 BCE. She wore similar clothes, although instead of a string skirt, hers was a long, square, woollen one that went down to her ankles. She wore a pair of large spiral earrings.

Skrydstrup Woman had an incredible hairdo, which involved all of her long, thick hair being combed forward over a hair pad and tied in place with cord, then intricately plaited across the forehead like a wreath, and covered with a hairnet of horse hair. Again, isotope analysis shows that she moved in her early teens from her place of origin, outside present-day Denmark, to Skrydstrup.

Traditional accounts often see these later prehistoric journeys as evidence for women moving from their distant homes to become part of their husband's family; what anthropologists call virilocality, from the Latin *virilis* meaning 'of a man'. This seems to me to reduce these girls' movements right down to almost nothing, so that they become passive objects, like pieces on a chess board. I'm not convinced. The science shows Egtved Girl toing and froing to different places late in her young life. Perhaps she was involved in long-distance transhumance, but I prefer to see these women on the move as pioneers and adventurers, filled with curiosity and wanderlust. After all, this is how male mobility is generally framed when there is comparable evidence for them in the archaeological record.

It's true that men and women have not always had equal freedom to move. At points in history, middle- and upper-class men have enjoyed less restriction than women. 'A man at least, is free,' wrote the French novelist Gustave Flaubert in *Madame Bovary* in 1857. 'He may travel over passions and over countries, overcome obstacles, taste of the most far-away pleasures. But a woman is always hampered.' But was this always the case? We must be careful about assuming that it applied equally in the deep past. Women throughout history didn't just sit passively at home waiting for their men, or hanging around to be married off to distant husbands; when they could, they were out there doing stuff. This might seem obvious to you or me, but you wouldn't believe how many interpretations of the past, even recent ones, seem like they were written by a heteronormative man from the 1950s, and contain more than a whiff of misogyny about them.

Women travellers in the Roman world were certainly perceived by contemporary authors as 'transgressive', but archaeology tells a different story. Evidence from inscriptions, artefacts and burials attests to the fact that Roman women of all ages and rank moved extensively. Likewise, analysis of later Viking burials shows that women were highly mobile. We find exotic and imported grave goods with both men and women, and while we don't know if this means people travelled or just the objects did, if we argue the case for men, as scholars have done, then we must also for women. This view of female mobility is backed up by both isotope and aDNA (ancient DNA) evidence from skeletons of this period, which show that as many women migrated as men.[1]

*

A similarly lazy assumption is that societies in the past were either mobile or sedentary, as if the two are mutually exclusive.

Hunter-gatherers in the vast timespan of the Palaeolithic and Mesolithic periods are often assumed to have been highly mobile, certainly compared with the societies that relied on farming from the beginning of the Neolithic period to the modern day.

This belief stems from economic function: hunter-gatherers move frequently to follow prey, while sedentary farmers do not. Hunter-gatherers must keep moving at the whim of nature, while farmers, having subdued and mastered their environment, control their mobility.

This view has persisted since at least the nineteenth century. In it, humans are understood as having emerged from a state of wandering wildness towards settled civilisation. According to this account, human progress can be measured by people's ability to settle down, move less, and exploit the landscape. Stasis becomes the norm and mobility an aberration.

But it's a fallacy. The anthropologist Hugh Brody highlights this stereotype in his book *The Other Side of Eden* and observes that it's quite often the wrong way around. 'It is agricultural societies that tend to be on the move; hunting people are far more firmly settled,' he says. Another anthropologist, Robert Kelly, agrees: 'Many hunter-gatherers move infrequently – some less than many "sedentary" horticultural societies.'[2]

Horticultural groups continue to move around: they still have to walk, and the larger the group, the further that has to be. And small-scale horticultural groups tend to carry on hunting and gathering to supplement their diet, only now their range needs to be bigger, which means walking further and for longer, and perhaps making use of a wider range of plants that require more processing. Small-scale horticulturalists also tend to move their residence regularly, either seasonally or every few years, as resources deplete. This involves abandoning their buildings for periods of time, or dismantling them completely and taking them with them. Keeping domesticated animals – as we have seen – also involves considerable movement throughout the year, living with them in different locations.

Farming requires changes to movement patterns, but not a cessation of them. It reorganises mobility, and in some cases actually increases it.

Through isotope analysis we can now archaeologically document movements of early farmers. This confirms that there was considerable relocation through people's lifetimes. The archaeological evidence now points to Neolithic farmers living a largely nomadic lifestyle, far from the settled farmers they were once believed to be. And over the last few decades archaeologists in Britain and Ireland have found evidence for really quite large, permanent buildings in the early part of the Mesolithic – buildings that anchored the supposedly drifting hunter-gatherers.[3]

Archaeology is only now beginning to pick up some of the nuances of people's movements. But mobility is still poorly understood, and it's difficult to see in the archaeological record, as noted elsewhere. Although we know movement is varied, complex and multi-dimensional, we struggle to identify that, and so just label groups as either mobile or settled. And because sedentism, being settled, is more easily seen – it leaves more archaeologically visible traces – we tend to recognise it, while any subtleties, like intermittent and oscillating sedentism, get conflated and just look permanent and long-term to us. Mobility is difficult to document; it's not an easy subject to study archaeologically.

But movement *is* variable, and history is not a one-way street from highly mobile to settled. There are gradations, and communities can increase mobility from one generation to the next, just as they can decrease it. Hunter-gatherers and early farmers alike had the capacity for self-creation and freedom; they had choices. Nothing tied them into a particular way of life. Like evolution, mobility is not linear but tangled and messy.

The ethnographic record is full of examples of communities whose movements swing between greater and lesser mobility. Some change throughout the same year with the seasons. Mobility can also vary hugely within the same community, and no matter how 'settled' a group may be, there are always segments that move around to a greater extent (as we all see in our own lives).[4]

Life has never been a simple division between static and mobile. We in the modern industrialised world are often supposed to be sedentary, but we have the highest mobility of any society at any time, using our cars, trains and planes to travel astonishing distances, at unprecedented velocities, effectively shrinking the world.

In this light, it seems odd that tension still exists between nomads and settled people; between Romany and Traveller groups, say, and the rest of society. If we take a long view, we see that this tension is misplaced, because we have always been mobile and settled, swinging fairly constantly between them.

Or maybe the tension isn't misplaced. Perhaps there has always been unease between those who move and those who stay. And perhaps there always will be.

12. WAYFARING:
BEING LOST AND LOSING
ONESELF

*In which we see the origin of the forest, climb
mountains, and wear fashionable clothing*

These days, when we use the word 'forest', we mean dense woodland. But a forest was originally, in medieval Britain at least, a legal term for an unfenced area, reserved for the Crown or its lessees, where deer were kept and hunted. This necessarily included woods, but was mainly heath, fen or moorland. It was an area outside the usual laws of the land, and subject to forest law, which protected the deer and supported the hunt. The word likely derives from the Latin *foris*, meaning 'outside' – 'foreign' has the same derivation. In this case, it means outside or external to the prevailing laws. So when we see, in historic documents or on modern interpretation panels, that, say, Pickering Forest once extended across the Vale of Pickering and up onto the North York Moors, that does not mean that in the medieval period a vast woodland existed across that whole area. It didn't. It was largely open moorland, just as Sherwood Forest was predominantly heathland.[1]

*

An abiding feature of much of northern Europe for the last few millennia, for many people, woodlands were a fundamental resource, from coppicing, trapping and charcoal-making, to gathering plants and fungi for their edibility and medicinal qualities. People have always been drawn to, and moved within, these rich worlds. For some now, and many in the past, woods represent home. Even outside the woodland itself, life in the past was immersed in wood – from handles of tools and furniture, to the houses that creaked and groaned and smelt of timber and forest life.

To move through, and live in, thick woodland is to be in close contact with animals and other beings; they are messy entanglements of people, the wood itself, and the multitudinous lives within it, all engaging with and attempting to make sense of one another, creating a web of living thoughts. Jam-packed full of meaning, they are loaded with myths and cautionary folktales, from Hansel and Gretel to Robin Hood. They permeate our dreams, and are repositories for vivid childhood memories of trees climbed and secret dens made.[2]

At times, woodlands can seem like impenetrable tangles of dense vegetation that might force people around them, or along their edges. But they are actually highly dynamic and variable, and movement through them is normally possible, even if it is a case of bushwhacking. Disturbances from fallen trees and grazing animals play a vital ecological role in creating openings and gaps in woodland. Glades such as these vary from place to place depending on topography, and they can create long, linear breaks, which form routes of travel.[3]

One of the major dangers in thick woodland is losing the path and getting lost, and even experienced navigators can lose their way. To do this is to find yourself in a dangerous other-place; one that you may not find your way back from.

As anyone who has been truly lost knows, it renders the environment immediately strange and alien, and is deeply disturbing. My terrible sense of direction means that I have experienced this feeling from time to time; in woods, on the moors, even walking down a busy high street with signposts to help direct me. I was lost for hours in thick woodland once when I was out mushroom-picking with my wife and a friend. Strangely, we only found the path again after a white stag appeared in front of us, like Harry Potter's Patronus Charm, and we decided to follow it.

But until the way out is found, to be lost is to be plunged into an unfamiliar world. Disorientation is distressing. Alone and undone, behaviour can easily become erratic – running, panicking, unthinking. To lose your way is to lose your head.[4] And it is when you are lost that you realise the landscape is far larger than you will ever know.

People who move regularly in unfamiliar landscapes learn the skill of being at home in the unknown. There is a difference to being lost and losing oneself, as the writer Rebecca Solnit has pointed out.[5] Losing yourself can be a form of discovery, a way of familiarising the unfamiliar:

'It is a surprising and memorable, as well as valuable, experience to be lost in the woods any time,' observed Henry David Thoreau in *Walden*.[6] To lose yourself is to lose track of time, immersed in your surroundings.

And it is through the act of willingly getting lost, and the subsequent discoveries, that humans came to colonise the planet.

Knowledge of the landscape is gained by roaming through it. In fact, it is *only* through this tentative path-making that an environment can be fully understood. For much of the past we haven't had maps, and it is ambulatory knowledge that allowed us to travel without them.[7]

The wayfarer is someone with this knowledge. By this, I don't mean a special person whose job it is to find the way, but anybody for whom travel on foot is a way of being. This will have been most people in the past, certainly in prehistory – and for much of historic times too. Maps, and now satnav, along with our general drift away from nature, make it hard to understand wayfaring, but this is how people in the past got around.

The wayfarer needs nothing external to tell them how to move from one place to another, for they understand their environment at an elementary level. This doesn't mean that they have a map in their head, because that would require a bird's-eye view of the world that until recently wasn't possible. Nor does it mean that they have a list of instructions in their mind before they leave – to turn this way, then that. The wayfarer understands the environment from the ground, which is their view of the world. Rather than knowing the route in advance, they discover it as they travel along the path, creating an act of continuous remembrance, much as musicians remember a song or a piece of music by playing it.[8]

Wayfarers are immersed in landscape in the same way that a tracker is immersed in the mind of the animal they are tracking, or a herder is with a herd. It is not navigation, but a way of 'feeling' around the landscape. By reading the land, a wayfarer can orient to the hills or trees, or the direction of a river. It is highly skilled, requiring close attention to surroundings, and using all of the senses – kinaesthetic, as well as sight, sound and smell. Wayfarers have a perceptual attunement to their world, and continuously adjust movements in response to surroundings.

Wayfarers use the shape and character of the land, and adjust according to the nature of the path, to the type of vegetation, to the hardness of the ground, to the presence of animals and birds, and to the light and sound around them. They understand the difference between the darker northern and sunnier southern slopes, and know that the North Star and Venus can guide walkers. The wayfarer adjusts their movements according to the shape and texture of trees, to leaves on the floor, puddles they step through, and the location of the sun and moon. Even to which side of the tree is greened with algae.

People in the past were alert to these things; they used their environment and the features in it to know their way around. The more varied the landscape, the easier it was. Their knowledge was the sum of all their movements, fine-tuned through the experience of trips previously made.[9]

*

Of course, people did, over time, find ways to record this knowledge. In the early medieval and later periods, it was customary to describe in detail the edges of a piece of land for legal reasons. These records are known as 'perambulations'; descriptions that were literally defined by walking. To take an example from near my home, the seventeenth-century Helmsley Estate boundary in North Yorkshire reads: 'From Lambe Folde Stones goeing N. to the Crosse with the Hande. And soe forward to Bagerstone leaveinge Cookinge Rigg beeing the land of the Lord Duke of Buckingham on the East. And so goeing N. wards upp Barney Gill to the Streete Way. Then turning N.W. to the bounder called Faceston ...', and so on.[10]

It's a sort of written form of map, and people could follow it, marking out the boundary limits. These boundaries could then be renewed regularly through people's feet, and, if necessary, perambulated by a jury to ensure no one had encroached onto the land. As a slight but interesting aside, by the eighteenth century the seasonal perambulation to fix territorial boundaries was undertaken by many people during the Ascension Day procession. This was usually led by a community representative accompanied by a group of children, and came to be known as the beating of the bounds.

The procession walked around the parish, village or manor bounds, halting at landmarks so that the children, and other recently arrived individuals, could be subjected to various types of painful hazing. If the landmark was a stream or a ditch, for example, a child might be tossed into it, or if it was a distinctive tree or boundary stone, they could be bumped against it, or held upside down. In this way, the children were unlikely to ever forget their boundaries should a dispute arise later in life.[11] Through personal physical contact with the land these boundaries were seared into their memory, and perpetuated for future generations. At the same time the villagers were incorporated into the collective identity of the territory the boundaries circumscribed, binding them and the land together.

Beating the bounds like this involved festivities and holidays too – eating, drinking and making merry – and this helped memories stick. It was also an important way of resisting enclosure, and villagers often carried tools for destroying hedges and fences with them.[12]

By the Victorian period this practice seems to have changed into a less painful performance, in which the boundaries were beaten out by the children using rods or staffs, so that rather than the landscape inscribing itself on them, the children inscribed themselves onto it.[13] This is a subtle but, I think, important change in our relationship to land, to one of dominance. One that we still have.

Either way, these boundaries were consolidated and renewed by each generation through their feet. The form of the land and the minds of the people inscribed themselves onto each other.

*

Some landscapes pose more treacherous obstacles to movement than others. Mountains, for example. Climbing is a different type of mobility altogether. It forces an estrangement from society, and can provide a sense of raw freedom, particularly on reaching the summit and seeing and feeling the emotion of the panorama. But it requires harder work than most movements, and contains greater dangers that focus the mind with each careful step.

Climbing uses hands as well as feet, requiring one to physically touch the environment; to feel one's way up the mountainside. In this sense it is more tactile and requires greater kinaesthetic awareness than other forms of movement, uniting the body and environment more intimately. As the climber moves up the rock face, the rock cuts into hands, wears down fingernails and bruises knees; inscribing itself onto the climber, just as the climber is inscribing him or herself onto it. Done often enough, and over time, the movement becomes second nature, and the climber's body is slowly transformed into a wiry, toughened 'climber's body'.[14] As we've seen, the skeleton is plastic and mouldable, and mobility and the land score themselves into the body.

In 1991, on a ridge in the Tyrolean Alps, a group of German hikers made a discovery: a body preserved in ice. Investigation established that the person, with an arrow still lodged in his shoulder, had died 5,000 years ago. (We don't know for sure that it was the arrow that killed him, but if it didn't, he would certainly have found it irritating.)

'Ötzi', as the Neolithic iceman came to be known – taking his name from a nearby valley – died around 3230 BCE. His soft tissue was preserved, enabling us to see at least 61 tattoos, and he was warmly dressed in three layers of clothing. He wore sheep leather leggings and loincloth, a soft chamois leather jacket, and a cape made of grass and bast fibre, the woody fibre that lines plant stems. His hat was bearskin. His shoes were insulated with grass and had bearskin soles and cattle leather uppers.[15]

The clothes were evidently kept in good condition, and they were sophisticated and entirely apposite for the environment. The same can be said for a beautifully decorated 2,300-year-old Scythian woman's leather boot, preserved in the Pazyryk region of the Altai Mountains in Siberia, which had pyrite crystals embedded into its sole to provide grip on the frozen ground – diamonds on the soles of her shoes,* as the song has it.[16]

*

Ever since footwear was invented, it has helped cleanse the contact between foot and ground, mediating the relationship between the two. Boots and shoes need to be 'broken in' to fit comfortably. Otherwise, their effect may be negative: interrupting and disrupting the flow of the walk, reducing or even halting our capacity to move.[17] The style of footwear also affects how we walk. Walking with soft-soled shoes, as people did for much of our past, creates a very different way of walking than we do now. It involves placing the ball of the foot down first, searching the ground, like a cat stalking a bird, rather than confidently plonking the heel down straight away with full weight, as we tend to do now with more solid soles. Try it at home – it's weirdly addictive, and really makes walking look quite different.

Soft leather soles do not stay watertight for long, and need frequent drying. Wooden pattens could be worn by

....

* I stole the 'diamonds on the soles of her shoes' line from a tweet by Prof. Susan Oosthuizen. Apologies, but it was too good to not include!

the wealthy to lift their feet above the mud (and literally raise them above the peasants), but for most working people it was normal to wear wet, chafing boots all day.

Like footprints, shoes recovered from archaeological sites can tell us a certain amount about the wearer, not least their foot size and therefore their likely age. Shoes are shaped by the wearer's feet too, and distinctive walking styles can be identifiable by wear patterns on them. It works both ways. The type of shoes a person wears can also mould the feet, as anyone who suffers from wearing high heels can probably testify. And that leaves an archaeological trace. Osteoarchaeological analysis of foot bones from a nineteenth-century farming community at Middenbeemster, in the Netherlands, showed repetitive trauma as a result of wearing shoes, in this case wooden clogs.

And we know that a fashion for extravagantly long and pointy shoes in fourteenth-century Britain led to an increase in foot problems. These shoes, known as poulaines or pikes, could reach truly eccentric proportions – the pointy tips becoming so long that they sometimes curled upwards, Blackadder-style. Some even had to be tied to the shins before they could be walked in. Analysis of medieval skeletons in Cambridge showed that this fashion was linked to an increase in bunions – a deformity of the big toe – as well as people tripping over and breaking bones.[18] The medieval pointy shoe was a fashion worn predominantly by the well-to-do (and, strangely, by friars) rather than the ordinary person. They were also a display of male sexuality in a society that linked foot size with penis size. For this reason, they were often worn in association with another phallic exaggeration: the padded codpiece.

In the City of London, I once excavated a pointy medieval leather shoe. As I took it from the ground and triumphantly held it aloft, a wad of moss fell out of the pointed end. Patrick, one of the older Irish men working on the building site, had been watching me. 'Oh!', he exclaimed. 'I used to do that with my winklepickers when I was a lad – except I used scrunched-up toilet paper to pad the end.' Plus ça change.

As this suggests, footwear and clothing more generally may always have been about more than just practical function. Whether they are fashionable, well-made or high-spec gives off information about the person on the move – are they a serious walker?, are they rich (literally well-heeled)?, and so on. In thirteenth-century Flanders only a noble could afford to flaunt their buttocks with a short doublet, a fashionable close-fitting jacket; as one fifteenth-century father counselled his son against them: 'They inflame women with lecherous desires.' Like a pilgrim, our clothes are part of our codified performance.[19]

Shoes and clothing shape movement more than we normally give them credit for, affording greater mobility within certain environments, and expanding the capacity of the human body.

And the land also shapes the walk; it determines the gait and the pace, whether to step carefully or stride confidently, whether to crawl or climb. The wrinkled hide of the landscape – with all its folds and creases, tangles and twists – has a habit of imposing itself upon the moving body.

PART 4

There and back again

13. ROADRUNNING: TRAVELLING THE SOCIAL REALM

In which we witness the development of the road and the invention of the wheel, and see how they've come to structure our lives

My father always loved the idea of the American open road. Many of my childhood holidays were spent driving in the States, never to anywhere in particular. Not really knowing what was around the bend, or over the crest. Or, if we had a destination, we didn't always arrive there. We would fly into whatever city we could get a ticket for, and strike out from there.

One year, we tried to make it to Yellowstone National Park, or perhaps it was Yosemite, but our slow, meandering

journey meant we ran out of time and stopped short. It didn't matter. We just tried again the following year. I don't now remember whether we ever actually made it, because it wasn't important; it was the journey that counted. Us, the family, moving across huge expanses of space. Getting lost in small towns with wide landscapes. We stayed in remote motels, cheap and chintzy. And we rarely took tourist routes. The landscape was boundless, and the road offered the promise of escape and new horizons.

Toad knew this when he exclaimed in *The Wind in the Willows*: 'The open road, the dusty highway, the heath, the common, the hedgerows, the rolling downs! Camps, villages, towns, cities! Here to-day, up and off to somewhere else to-morrow! Travel, change, interest, excitement! The whole world before you, and a horizon that's always changing!'

The road sits large in our collective minds.

Walt Whitman celebrated the American open road, and the road was a metaphor that defined the Beat Generation of 1950s America, from Jack Kerouac's *On the Road* to John Steinbeck's *Travels with Charley*. For both Kerouac and Steinbeck, the road trip was a search for knowledge; a quest to understand the world. For Thelma and Louise in Ridley Scott's film of that name the road represented freedom from oppressive patriarchal society. And for the father and son in Cormac McCarthy's *The Road* it represented an unknown destination where survival might be only a possibility.[1]

Roads can feel like unanchored space. Free from society, rules, or one's self; a majestic space of possibility. Roads conjure up romantic notions of rebellious free spirits. Transcendence and transgression.

Some or all of these qualities can be glimpsed in powerful images of roads, whether photographs of tarmac narrowing into a fine point on the horizon or the gentler curling movement in the watercolours of – to name just one of many – the early twentieth-century painter Eric Ravilious: tracks, paths, roads, sometimes viewed from a hillside or a moving train.

*

Every schoolchild knows that the Roman road network transformed much of Britain – an advanced system imposed on an unsuspecting prehistoric world, the tentacles of a grand empire. *Monty Python* taught us that much. 'What have the Romans ever done for us?', Reg asks of the People's Front of Judea in the film *The Life of Brian*. 'The roads?', comes one answer. 'Well, yeah, obviously the roads. I mean the roads go without saying, don't they?'

Why wouldn't the Romans have brought the roads with them? After all, they introduced so much else ('Apart from the sanitation, the medicine, education, wine, public order, irrigation, roads, a fresh water system, and public health, what have the Romans ever done for us?'). But archaeological evidence is always emerging and dating techniques evolve. It is now clear that Roman roads owe much to pre-existing routes. In fact, we know that Iron Age societies had properly engineered roads in Britain, not just worn tracks and paths.

Traces of this early road system have been there for a while. A Late Iron Age street grid, with cobbled surfaces, lies under the Roman town of Silchester, and similar evidence has been excavated at the Iron Age hillfort of Danebury, both in Hampshire. Simple Iron Age roads are known to cross the Yorkshire Wolds.

The clearest evidence for a proper Iron Age road in Britain is at Sharpstone Hill near Shrewsbury in Shropshire. Here, in 2009, several phases of a well-engineered and maintained road were excavated in advance of the extension of a quarry – where, oddly, hundreds of thousands of tonnes of aggregate, prized for its grippiness, is quarried each year to surface modern roads in Britain and Formula One tracks around the world. The ancient Iron Age road had been carefully engineered with a cambered construction (meaning that the surface sloped down from the centre to drain off excess water), and used compacted river pebbles to form a hard surface. The road had been laid over a mat of elder brushwood, which itself followed an earlier routeway used for droving cattle. On either side of the road were drainage ditches. Without scientific dating this would no doubt have been described as a typical Roman road. But both radiocarbon and OSL dating demonstrated that it was built in the Iron Age before the Roman conquest. This road did not lead to Rome. Similar roads undoubtedly linked large Iron Age settlements, known as oppida.[2]

The road at Sharpstone Hill had a Roman road constructed over the top of it, and one wonders how many other Roman roads were actually constructed over earlier ones. Quite a lot, I suspect, and as more roads are excavated and scientific dating techniques are applied to them, we will start to see an established Iron Age road system.

To have imposed a complete network upon a country would require the road to have been conceived in a vacuum and then parachuted onto a blank landscape. That clearly did not happen. Roads are not made; they *emerge* from people's movements on the ground. They gain, then lose, importance. They're altered to meet ever-changing needs, organically and iteratively, on the ground. Each new stage is tacked on to what was there before. A similar process occurred in colonial North America with road-building over ancient, pre-colonial trails and highways, such as Broadway in New York City, which partly overlies the Wickquasgeck trail. Perhaps the roads my father drove us on, years ago, were originally walked into being by Native Americans, long before Columbus. Even modern motorways that don't follow existing routes nevertheless follow the topography and avoid settlements, or divert around significant places in the landscape, sometimes after losing hard-fought battles with protesters. This happened at Otmoor near Oxford where campaigners bought a field in the middle of the proposed route of the M40, divided it up into thousands of small plots and sold them, making it all but impossible for the government to compulsorily buy the land. Roads develop on the ground to solve specific problems. They always have an undercurrent of history.

Having established that Britain had routeways, trackways and, occasionally, roads before the Romans came, we can acknowledge that Roman roads were qualitatively different. They altered the capacity to speed around the country and access new areas. They felt different beneath the feet.

But the first Roman roads were quite modest, and it took a while to create what we know as the Roman road network.

Archaeological evidence is plentiful. Roman roads were well made and suited all weathers. Sometimes they were built on an artificial bank, called an 'agger', on which the metalled surface rested; raising the road up so that it literally became a highway. Drainage ditches on either side kept the road dry. In a rainy place like Britain this is essential. The metalling generally comprised a foundation of larger stones overlaid with cobbles or gravel, to form a smooth running surface. This was often deliberately compacted – although in reality the passage of people, animals and vehicles would have done this too – providing a smooth, hard layer, which must have provided a different experience of moving to what went before.

The surface often had a slight camber from the centre to the edge, just like the Iron Age Sharpstone Hill road. That said, there was no special formula for roads, and they varied considerably depending on the requirements of the route and the local soils. For example, on well-drained ground there was no need for an agger, or indeed any roadside ditches. Their design and construction developed, quite literally, from the ground up.

Contrary to popular myth, Roman roads were not always dead straight. That would have required an aerial view of the world that – as I've said before – did not exist at the time. The main Roman roads are generally direct, but they do not slavishly follow a straight line, regardless of terrain. Roman surveyors were experts in their field, finding solutions to moving around and creating connections within the landscape. They avoided obstacles, considered geology, and deviated to cross rivers at appropriate points, or to ensure minimum numbers of crossings. All of which required local knowledge.[3]

The things we now call Roman roads were the trunk roads: the motorways of the day. But the vast majority of Roman roads were actually minor roads that meandered just as they do now. In fact, they probably form the basis for some of today's minor roads. Studying Roman roads at the broad scale – as lines on maps – enhances the appearance of straightness, and emphasises their efficiency. I prefer the on-the-ground perspective afforded to archaeologists, which shows a different picture, with small localised twists and turns.

For the well-known straight sections of Roman road, it may be that the Romans optimised routes that were already there, strengthening and straightening, smoothing out bends and corners. Much later, turnpike surveyors did the same. And it's possible that even the prehistoric routes may have been reasonably straight, having themselves been based on long-lived (and modified) movements. We can see this at Sharpstone Hill, where the Iron Age road lies over an earlier route.

Cut through a Roman road in larger urban areas, as I have done, and you will see the stratigraphy that makes up the road, including amendments and changes, adjustments and tweaks. I still remember the joy of finding filled-in potholes, as well as resurfacing layers sitting on top of older surfaces, when I excavated a section of Roman road in Southwark in London. It reminded me of the patchwork of tarmacked surfaces in the country lanes of my childhood – the bits you are not supposed to see.

All this is to say that roads grow out of the landscape they are developed for. They are palimpsests: accumulations over time.

*

At the opening of a new road in Samoa, the writer Robert Louis Stevenson said: 'Our road is not built to last a thousand years. Yet in a sense it is ... When a road is once built, it is a strange thing how it collects traffic, how every year as it goes on, more and more people are found to walk thereon, and others are raised up to repair and perpetuate it, and keep it alive; so that perhaps even this road of ours may, from reparation to reparation, continue to exist and be useful hundreds and hundreds of years after we are mingled in the dust.'

Roman roads in Britain endured longer than Roman rule, and influenced much later history here. If a Roman road is still in use today – and many are – that's because it has been in continuous use since its construction.

A road soon degrades if it is not used. Unmetalled roads would flood in low-lying areas, washing away soil and turning clay to mud, while feet, hooves and wheels would have done considerable damage over time. Freezing and thawing of the ground throughout the winter and early spring would have cracked and broken up the compacted gravel surface of disused Roman roads. Weeds would quickly grow in these cracks and widen them further. Within a few decades they would have been overgrown with vegetation and impassable. A century later we might expect thorn bushes to grow on the road, perhaps a small wood.

Rudyard Kipling captures this, and the ghostly sense of what was there before, in his poem 'The Way Through the Woods' from 1910.

They shut the road through the woods
Seventy years ago.

Weather and rain have undone it again,
And now you would never know
There was once a road through the woods ...

Yet, if you enter the woods
Of a summer evening late,
When the night-air cools on the trout-ringed pools ...
You will hear the beat of a horse's feet,
And the swish of a skirt in the dew ...

*

It seems highly likely that the medieval world had a sophisticated and well-maintained road network, whether or not it remains visible now. And not just roads they inherited but new roads they brought into use.

The deserted medieval villages we saw earlier contain in their layout fossilised evidence for medieval roads. In mid-Wales, there's a medieval road, the Monk's Trod, that connected two twelfth-century abbeys. There are other Monk's Trods, and a Monk's Walk, in the North York Moors. These were most likely used to transport wool on horseback. In fact, an extensive network of these 'trods' traversed the moors here. They were generally made of flagstones around half a metre wide, and were used to move commodities across the moors, either from markets or from the big producers, such as monasteries, or by panniermen to carry fish inland from coastal villages to York and elsewhere. Smaller trods linked to mills, churches and farms.[4]

Some are still visible; others were destroyed by landowners. I love searching out trods on the moors and following them. I spread out our dog-eared OS map on the dining room table, and plan – like a military leader in a war room – a walk, ideally one that takes me within striking distance of a pub. (And I love the word 'trod'. It defines what you do on them. We tread along a trod, just as we ride along a road, and drive cattle along a drove.)

Other roads emerged in the medieval period too, particularly on a local scale, and between new towns and villages. These winding and unmetalled roads were not constructed or engineered like Iron Age or Roman roads, but came into use through habitual movement and routine lines of travel. Like the prehistoric routes before them, they became manifest if used a lot, but disappeared quickly if not.

They were living ways, 'easements', rather than physical entities. These rights of way were protected by legislation. Travellers could, by law, diverge from the route if it became obstructed or 'founderous' in wet weather. This is why you sometimes see multiple parallel routeways in the countryside. Aerial photographs frequently reveal evidence of where a road fanned out into parallel tracks created by medieval trippers moving from side to side as the way became blocked or flooded.

Roads were, as they still are, social spaces that channelled diverse groups of people, where they could mingle as they moved.

Roman roads were used principally by the military to move foot soldiers, riders and freight carts, as well as by the official postal service. Medieval armies used much the same network. It used to be thought that in the Saxon period *herepaths* (literally 'army paths') were military roads, but it's likely they were used more broadly, linking important sites such as 'hundred' meeting places. Also known as a 'moot', hundreds were assembly sites where the wealthy and powerful men of the territorial unit known as a 'hundred' met and discussed local issues, and where judicial trials were held. These sites were typically at crossroads or fords in a river.

Integral to medieval and post-medieval roads were the grassy verges, known as the 'long acre'. This was an important piece of common land on which farmers would tether livestock for grazing – either drovers on long journeys, or local farmers moving livestock from one field to another.[5]

Other travellers along medieval roads included almost every section of society. Traders and merchants with rumbling carts or loaded packhorses. Wandering minstrels who, for a small fee, could play a merry jig on their pipe or rebec. Travelling justices, sheriffs and revenue collectors. Outlaws haunted the main roads, such as the Folville and Coteral gangs who in the fourteenth century roamed forest roads looking for travellers to rob, murder and rape. For this reason it paid to travel in groups for protection, meeting up at inns with others taking the same road. Messengers too were frequent users of the road because – well, movement is knowledge. Pilgrims of course frequented the roads, as did itinerant preachers, friars and bishops moving through their chains of estates.

Royal courts, throughout the Middle Ages, were largely itinerant. Queens and kings moved constantly to keep in contact with all parts of their realm, in travelling circuses of authority and majesty, comprising a baggage train of carts, wagons and packhorses, as well as household knights and squires, sergeants-in-arms, servants, valets and boys.

As chancellor of England, Thomas Becket travelled with 200 household members in 1158. Harbingers went ahead of these entourages in order to organise accommodation. Local people acted as guides, providing advice on directions and best routes. This sort of nobility mobility provided an exciting spectacle, and no doubt attracted others to the road – rubber-neckers, the sick and needy looking for handouts, pick-pockets and prostitutes.[6]

Administrative accounts carefully itemise the expenses required for these journeys and indicate the huge size of the baggage trains, but there is little evidence in the archaeological record; though a late fifteenth-century travelling chest of Lady Margaret Beaufort, mother of Henry VII, can be seen on display in Westminster Abbey.

Moving in large groups like this, as we've noted before, was an opportunity to be seen: the stateliness was designed to be noticed. People could recognise at a glance their place in the hierarchy. Still today, heads of state put on a preening show during state visits such as a G7 summit. It seems reasonable to conjecture that far back in prehistory rulers of any kind will have done something similar.

*

If a route is used by the same groups often enough for specific purposes, it can take on associations with them. Routes and roads to churches, religious shrines and other places of importance sometimes take on the association with their destination, and become themselves sacred, ceremonial or ritual.

Corpse roads – also known as bier roads, coffin roads, funeral roads, lyke ways or lych ways – were used in the medieval and later periods to transport the dead, along with any funeral party, to the nearest licensed burial ground, which in remote areas could be some miles over the countryside. One last journey before the final resting place. Sometimes corpse roads included 'coffin stones' beside the path, to accommodate a coffin or shrouded corpse while pall-bearers took a rest. These roads tended to accumulate special significance in folk tales of ghosts and processions of spirits: roads for cavalcades of corpses and gatherings of ghosts.[7] We can see something of this in one of Puck's soliloquies in Shakespeare's *A Midsummer Night's Dream*:

Now it is the time of night
That the graves all gaping wide,
Every one lets forth his sprite,
In the churchway paths to glide.

Crossroads seem to have always been interesting places too. We saw in an earlier chapter how some Neolithic henge monuments may have been constructed at, or developed out of, crossroads. Markers, stone crosses and statues of saints were often placed at crossroads in the medieval period as landmarks for travellers. The place where traffic converges is clearly a good spot to advertise certain messages, and reach wide audiences.

Execution sites were also often located at crossroads, such as the famous Tyburn gallows in London, from at least the twelfth century through to the early eighteenth, at the junction of two Roman roads (now Edgware Road and

Oxford Street). Criminals, deviants and social outcasts were sometimes buried at crossroads; and it's not surprising that crossroads attracted stories of witches, ghosts and magic. And suicide victims, generally after the body had been dragged through the streets and mocked, perhaps also staked through the heart, were buried at crossroads. Remarkably, this burial practice continued from the medieval period until the Burial of Suicide Act of 1823 abolished it.

Burying people at crossroads acknowledged that these were liminal spaces, where journeys change direction and decisions must be made. The spirits of people buried there would – it was hoped – be puzzled into indecision and therefore immobility. It's curious, then, that enslaved people were sometimes ceremonially freed at crossroads.[8]

*

Compared with roads, and the detailed evidence of their construction, it's harder to find evidence of vehicles in the archaeological record.

The wheel, beloved by *The Far Side* comic strip and *The Flintstones* cartoons, in which they are usually depicted as chunkily-made and hewn from stone, is seen as one of humanity's great inventions. Like fire. Or sliced bread.

But the wheel actually arrived fairly late in prehistory, during the Copper Age in Mesopotamia and Europe. Archaeological evidence suggests that wheels developed around 3500 BCE, and were made of wood, not stone. Soon after this time, we find quite good evidence for wheels, in written Mesopotamian records, as images incised on the surface of pots, or in little clay models of wheeled wagons in eastern and central Europe. Cart tracks uncovered beneath a long barrow at Flintbek in northern Germany provide archaeologists with another clue to wheels dated to around 3400 BCE.

From around 3300 and 3200 BCE, we find actual wheels on small wooden wagons preserved under burial mounds known as kurgans, in the steppe grasslands of Russia and Ukraine, or preserved in bogs and lakes in the Alpine regions of Switzerland and Germany.[9]

The reason for this relatively late development is that wheels are actually phenomenally complicated. They are part of a complex combination of different moving and load-bearing parts, including the requirement for an axle to hold the vehicle. And these need to fit perfectly together: too tight and the wheel will not move; too loose and it wobbles.

Wheels led to major advances including haulage of heavy things that could previously only be carried efficiently on water: wood, or clay for pottery, food for humans and animals, animals themselves, and their skins and hides. Plus, of course, people.

Wheeled vehicles must have changed human movement beyond recognition. And what a vision to see, for the very first time, wagons pulled by oxen rolling by. Or, later, the first chariots charging past, pulled by horses and driven by warriors wielding spears or firing arrows.

In the British Isles, the earliest evidence for the wheel comes from the Middle and Late Bronze Age, around 1300 BCE, where a handful of fragmentary examples are preserved at waterlogged sites, such as Flag Fen near Peterborough, and at Cottenham near Cambridge. The biggest and most complete found to date comes from Must Farm – that well-preserved site in the Fens we visited earlier. The Must Farm wooden wheel dates to around 1000 BCE, measures a metre in diameter, and would have been part of a two-person cart. It was made using three large wooden boards held together by two wooden bracers. In the middle is an axle made of oak.

A few centuries later, chariots and carts accompanying burials are known from Middle Iron Age cemeteries, particularly in eastern Yorkshire. These vehicles are usually neatly dismantled and stacked in the grave alongside the deceased, presumably a cherished and high-status possession from life, ready and waiting to transport the dead in the afterlife. One recently excavated in Pocklington, at the foot of the Yorkshire Wolds, was found complete and erect, with the owner lying in the cart on his shield. Even more amazing was that in the grave were the skeletons of two upright horses looking as if they were pulling the cart. The horses had been killed prior to burial (for a while it was thought that they were buried alive), and placed in a sort of leaping action, presumably as rigor mortis was setting in, as if dragging the cart, and its owner, up to the heavens. The horses' skulls were missing when they were excavated, and so it is quite possible that their heads stuck up above ground in some sort of freakish gesture.

*

Travel by car throws up its own distinctive form of movement. It has opened up huge swathes of the landscape to visit, and a new world of choice and opportunity. In the bubble of our own car we may feel disengaged from the world around us. But no movement is ever entirely separate from the landscape in which it takes place. The bumps and turns of the roads are the same for a car, and its driver, as they were for any cart or carriage in the past.

People have always been vulnerable on the road, whether from wild animals, other people, or some other threat. Where once the great fear may have been highwaymen, the combustion engine brings menace that is slower to hurt, such as toxic exhaust and climate change, as well as the instantaneous, swift danger of high-speed collision. For most of us, now, driving on the road is likely to be the most dangerous thing we do. I know that only too well. Perhaps you do too.

It's hardly surprising that, as well as building physical roads, we have constructed an increasingly elaborate complement of laws, rules and written codes to follow: codified messages for those in the know, much like the ones we glimpsed in other epochs. As well as these formal codes, there are informal ones. As in any other social space, we deliver messages, consciously and unconsciously, as we pass through. Cars are a conspicuous display of wealth, fashion, style, comfort, safety or sexual competitiveness (delete as appropriate to you!).[10] More consciously, we message other travellers with angry honking or insolent gestures out of the window, or – more often, I think – by instances of kindness and civility such as flashing to allow another ahead of us, or a raised hand to say thank you.

It's likely that some version of these codes, whether formal or informal, has always applied to road users.

*

Road building is political. People living nearby often campaign vigorously against it, worried about pollution, noise, danger and the destruction of particular wildlife habitats. Meanwhile, developers lobby the government for more road building. As I write this, a long-standing argument about the road that runs alongside Stonehenge, and how to bypass it, has flared up once again, and neither side of this particularly brutal battleground seems to appreciate that the road itself has a history and has developed out of the landscape, just as the prehistoric monuments have.

To an archaeologist, road building represents a valuable opportunity to find archaeological sites. I cut my teeth working on road schemes, among other developments and infrastructure projects. On one, in Wiltshire, we found extraordinarily rare evidence for one of our early ancestors, probably *Homo heidelbergensis*, dated to around 375,000 years ago. This took the form of dozens of flint hand-axes, in mint condition, as well as the bones of a small relative of the modern horse that had been hunted and butchered. On another road project, in east London, I excavated a length of Bronze Age wooden trackway that had been preserved in the peat, formed long ago in the marshy areas around the River Lea. An ancient trackway found by the construction of a modern roadway; 3,500 years of human mobility bumping up against one another.

*

Despite their obvious association with movement, when viewed as history or archaeology, paths, tracks and roads tend to be thought of as passive, static artefacts. To me, they are anything but inert. Roads act on us as much as we act on them. They collect us up, and channel us along.

14. FLOWING: JOURNEYING WITH THE FERRYMAN

In which we see rivers providing a different way of moving, and cities orienting to their flow

At some point, a road will have to cross a river. These pinch points – whether ferry, ford or bridge – are supreme gathering places, forcing people together and creating unique social spaces.

Fords were ubiquitous across British rivers, and many still survive, either physically, or as a place-name suffix. Bedford, Stratford, Hereford, Hertford, and so on. Twyford, of which there are a few in the UK, means that there were two river crossings. Stanford means a ford constructed with stones, while the name Oxford tells us both that there was once a ford through the river, and the type of animals driven across it. My personal favourite are the places ending in -wade; Biggleswade in Bedfordshire, for example, or Iwade in Kent. Wade is a highly descriptive – immersive even – word for ford. It does what it says on the tin!

From at least the Roman period, these shallow points in the river were occasionally laid with gravels or flat stones to provide a hard surface for feet, hooves and wheels to trundle over. Where the river was too deep to wade across, cable ferries and ferrymen could be used, and these are recorded in written history.

The strategic value of crossing places is recorded in the *Anglo-Saxon Chronicle*, a collection of copied manuscripts, the originals dating from the ninth to twelfth centuries CE. In one powerful image, we see Edward the Elder, king of the Anglo-Saxons, meeting the Danish king of East Anglia and Northumbria for a horseback parley in 906, in the middle of the river that divided their territories.[1]

In prehistory, people probably relied on fords and stepping stones for crossing narrow waterways. One can imagine prehistoric ferries for the wider stretches. And there is solid evidence from the Bronze Age for another way of crossing rivers: bridges.

At Vauxhall in London, not far from the postmodernist MI6 building, a constant scouring of the foreshore by the Thames has revealed parallel rows of posts. First noticed in 1993 and monitored since, these have been shown to be Bronze Age in date and once would have supported a raised walkway. This footbridge spanned part of the river to a gravel island that then existed in the middle of the Thames, and from there to the other side. Similar wooden piles, representing the remains of bridges, have been recorded across a former channel of the Thames at Dorney in Buckinghamshire. And the remains of three Middle Bronze Age bridges were excavated on a building site outside Southampton. These are Britain's earliest known bridges.

Fords and bridges gather the landscape, funnelling people and animals to cross a waterway at a single point.[2] They are intensely social, important trading places that in the past provided merchants and traders with ready access to travellers. It is no wonder that these crossing points often became settlements, the foundation of towns, and the places where roads converge. From the medieval period, some urban bridges were covered in houses and shops, with markets at the ends or even (if there was room) on the bridge itself.

Control the bridge and you control the road. Control the road and you control the people who use it. Of course, that process of control isn't always peaceful: just think of King Harold's army meeting Norwegian invaders, in 1066, at the Battle of Stamford Bridge. In the later Middle Ages, bridges on the continent were fortified and in Britain defensive gateways were built on them, or nearby.

Like roads, bridges have entered popular consciousness as powerful metaphors, ambiguous spaces between stark contrasts (life and death, good and evil), providers of safe passage over troubled water, and frightening thresholds (in stories, there might be a troll hiding beneath them). This ambiguity has lent them – like crossroads – profoundly spiritual connotations.

Hermits often positioned themselves next to bridges, drawn by their liminality. From the fourteenth century onwards, hermits became increasingly responsible for the upkeep of bridges, paid for with the donations and pledges they received. They even sometimes performed repairs themselves. Road and bridge upkeep was, after all, pious work, for it kept pilgrims moving. The point at which Watling Street crossed the River Darent at Dartford (note the suffix) – the first stop out of London on this pilgrim route to Canterbury – had a 'hermit of the ford' from at least the thirteenth century until the sixteenth (different people, obviously). The hermit conducted people across the river and, later, after a footbridge had been built, collected alms for bridge repairs.

By the fourteenth century, indulgences were often granted to anyone who contributed to bridge construction and upkeep. Bridge chapels, built throughout the Middle Ages, offered Mass early in the morning to allow travellers to worship before taking to the roads. Bridge chapels were built across, or at one end or one side of, the bridge, and occasionally they were built on an island in the river.[3]

Over long periods of time, crossing places can themselves move, or become abandoned, as the river changes, bridges fall, and new ones are built. This in turn diverts and reconfigures the network of paths and roads around them, sometimes disrupting entire settlements that had relied on the previous routes and their traffic. The above-mentioned Biggleswade is a case in point. An early medieval routeway provided a direct route into the town's marketplace, crossing the River Ivel at a ford (the 'wade' that gave the town its name). But later, possibly in the twelfth century, a stone bridge was built some distance to the north, causing a fundamental reconfiguration of traffic, and therefore to parts of the town itself. Old roads were abandoned and new ones built.[4] We see something similar today, when bypass roads are constructed around towns and cities, causing shops and other commercial enterprises to lose passing trade.

*

Up to now, we've focused on terrestrial travel. But rivers are not just obstacles to be crossed. They run through our minds as much as they thread our landscapes, providing a sense of place as well as a source of memories, from playing on the banks to wild swimming. They help shape our world by creating boundaries. Many a village, parish or county perimeter follows a river, as any number of 'perambulations' will tell you. Rivers keep people apart, but also attract us to them – along with other animals and birds looking for water – so that riverbanks become gathering points, as clearly shown by the archaeology.[5]

People attune themselves to the flow of the river; its force provides an axis of movement: an upstream or downstream that makes it easier moving in one direction than the other. And throughout history, towns and cities oriented themselves to this flow. This generates its own rhythms, as well as identities and communities. Take any medieval city – London, York, wherever – and you will see that the line of the river and its tributaries once provided the orientations of the main roads, which ran parallel and perpendicular to them. This influenced the patterns of streets and houses, and, later, sewerage systems integrated with the rivers. Industries were drawn to the river: fisheries with their weirs and fish traps, or reed-cutters and basket-makers for proximity to their resources. Away from houses and near to the water, stinking tanneries were to be found, and breweries, and noisy mills and forges.

Rivers are part of sacred geographies and there are countless examples of belief in river spirits and river gods, and of the sacred and supernatural role of rivers. Rivers such as the Ganges and Yamuna in India are venerated as deities, and for good reason – they provide fresh, life-giving water, and irrigate the northern Indian plains, and we've seen how they draw millions of people for the Kumbh Mela festival. The Jordan, in Israel, is where baptism by water provided a new life to early Christians.

Revered for sustaining life, there's also something fearful and mysterious about the force and unseen depths of rivers and lakes. In early Christian literature, bodies of water were often portrayed as holding great danger, and journeying on water was an ordeal of faith.[6] Rivers were regularly used in the past to dispose of the dead too, and in some countries still are. They are death-receiving as well as life-giving.

In British prehistory, water was likely used in a wide range of cleansing and purification rituals. As we've seen, there's a connection between Neolithic henge monuments and rivers, and it's no coincidence that rivers run past the major monuments of British prehistory. Accumulations of Mesolithic and Neolithic stone axe-heads have been found at various places along the River Thames, with concentrations in the wide meanders in west London, a tradition that continued through the metal ages, with echoes in later history.[7] With no written sources to guide us, we can't know for sure why they were deposited there, but perhaps these stone axes were thrown in the same way that Romans tossed coins into rivers, to placate the river god – not unlike the way we flip coins into wells, and other watery places, to make a wish.

As natural routeways for water, rivers play a vital role in movement for people and technology. In wet and watery landscapes, waterways become highways. While ridgeways have dominated past discussions of long-distance movement in prehistory, the role of rivers and movement on them – so familiar to us in modern times – has often been overlooked. Before the coming of the canals and railways, rivers were the principal means of transporting goods; and in prehistory people, animals and materials travelled along rivers, estuaries and coasts, and across the seaways around Britain, facilitating the dissemination of things and ideas. Rivers provided a national network of long-distance contacts, penetrating into most parts of the land, the extent of which has undoubtedly been underestimated.

Time is experienced differently on water, so that water travel seems to occupy its own temporal zone. To people whose only prior experience of moving was on foot, water travel must have seemed to bring places much closer together.

To take a specific example: prehistoric canoeists. In the preserving soils of Must Farm quarry, where, as we've seen, a Bronze Age settlement (and a wheel) was discovered near Peterborough, nine log boats were also excavated. These dugout canoes, made from single tree trunks, hollowed out, were found within a stretch of a prehistoric river channel that once meandered across that part of the Cambridgeshire Fens. These log boats would have been ideal for the gentle pace of river travel in the flat fenland landscapes, paddling or punting them up or downstream.

Elsewhere the physical evidence for later prehistoric canoes is extraordinarily rare, with just the remains of a handful of other examples discovered around England: a dozen or so canoes or fragments of them from the Bronze Age, and around the same again from the Iron Age. Scant as the evidence is, the existence of these rudimentary boats reminds us that the waterways of prehistoric Europe were likely bustling with activity.

15. WEATHERSCAPE: OF SKIES AND SEASONS

In which weather and seasons bake and batter our lives and alter our movements

None of the movements in this book happen with a neutral sky above and around them. It is sometimes scorching and sometimes freezing. There is fog and mist, and rain and storms. And these affect the way one moves. Events happen under scudding skies.

When we take a moment to remember that, we see more clearly the movements of our predecessors: we see that the promenades in Paris probably stopped when it snowed; that Chaucer's pilgrims were wise to wait until April before setting off from London to Canterbury; and that Ötzi must have thought carefully about his clothing before venturing out over the mountains of the Tyrol.

You can't escape weather – it is everywhere, and always. And it brings variance to routes and paths. Flooded roads, or snowed-in mountain passes, made a considerable difference to the way people moved. Weather alters light and temperature, and transforms the texture of our paths.

And yet hardly anyone ever talks about seasons or weather in archaeology, particularly in prehistory. By ignoring it, we effectively deny any sort of differences in lived experience, as if everything in the past happened in one homogenous, weatherless day. We rarely even acknowledge days and nights, or the way the sun moves across the sky. This is odd, because archaeologists, like gardeners, spend an inordinate amount of time outdoors, and in all weathers. During fieldwork we become expert weather-watchers, obsessing about approaching clouds, and trying to predict the next downpour.

To be fair, weather, like movement, is difficult to pick up in archaeology. We can only imagine prehistoric people squinting and shading their eyes from the sun. We cannot trace numb hands, chapped fingers and watering eyes. But we know these things must have happened.

This is not the same as changing climate, by the way, which can be, and frequently is, recorded within archaeology.[1] Weather is more instantaneous – a mountain blast, or a sea breeze.

To address this weather-blindness in archaeology, it is worth thinking through how weather manifests and is experienced in our own lives – not just freakish events, but everyday weather too – and then applying it to the archaeological record. As an example of our own weather experience, think of the joy of petrichor – the smell of rain hitting warm, dry earth. This is a word derived from the Greek *petra*, meaning stone, and *ichor*, which, in Greek mythology, is the blood of the gods. Proof that we *can* get blood from a stone. Beautiful things require beautiful words. And what can be more wonderful than psithurism, the gentle whisper of leaves rustling in the wind? To archae-ologists who spend so much time outdoors, these words furnish us with a deeper sense of the place we're exploring.

The way weather is experienced, and – which is differ-ent – the way it is understood by people, shapes the way they move through a landscape. It's often said that the past happened 'under a different sky'. Well, it didn't! We are under the same sky and despite different climates we feel the same weather as our predecessors, although they will have made sense of it differently. Weather was cer-tainly felt by the Roman soldiers stationed on Hadrian's Wall. Letters written on sheets of wood in the first and second centuries CE and excavated from Vindolanda, an auxiliary fort along Hadrian's Wall in Hexham, attest to that. One letter talks about enduring 'troublesome' storms, while another, sent to someone stationed on the wall, tells the recipient: 'I have sent you ... pairs of socks ... and two pairs of underpants.' The cold wind does have a habit of whistling up the tunic in those parts.

Sometimes the 'archaeological record' of weather, or temperature, is written into the landscape through place-names – Cold Blow in the south-west of Wales, for example, or the amusing-sounding Windy Bottom near Lantern Pike Hill in Derbyshire. North America is replete with weather-related place-names, from Sunnyvale and Seabreeze in Texas to Breezy Point and Good Thunder in Minnesota. But of course, we have more than just these names to go on. Archaeological evidence taken from sed-iment deposits in Cape Cod shows that extraordinarily powerful hurricanes pounded New England during the first millennium CE.

We can only wonder how people in the past made sense of those storms, the thunderclaps and lightning forks, clouds and rainbows, the breathtaking magnitude of the night sky. The moon can be a companion, lighting the way on a dark night, and the stars our fellow travellers. But how else might these things have been understood?

Did prehistoric societies, like Shakespeare, use weather as a metaphor – to express passion, turmoil or foreboding? Did Neolithic mythology incorporate some version of *The Tempest*'s howling winds, or *Romeo and Juliet*'s stifling heat? Weather is a key element in Greek, Roman and Norse mythology, a token of the gods' assorted fickle whims. For some Australian aboriginal groups, rainbows are malevolent serpents, for others the Rainbow Snake is the Creator and when it appears in the skies it is thought to be moving from one waterhole to another. It was said that the sixth-century Irish monk Columba, who we shall meet again later in the book, could control the winds; and this was certainly understood as a gift from God. Columba lived and died on the tiny Scottish island of Iona, a place well known to be stormy; a small and unoccupied offshore island next to Iona is still known as the Island of Storm.

Like landscape, weather carries layers of meaning – rarely thought about when discussing archaeology – whether that is divine (bad weather is often seen as a punishment from God) or made up of personal memories and moods (perhaps brought on by seasonal affective disorder).[2]

*

As well as momentary instances of weather, we must consider the rhythm of the changing seasons. Days extend and shorten, light grows and fades in strength, and in consequence journeys get longer and shorter. The seasons dominated life in the past.[3]

Travelling conditions improve in spring, and this was when past societies headed out on the road again, as we saw with the pilgrimages. In the medieval period it was also a time for hunting, hawking and jousting for the royal court and the nobility. March, named after Mars, the Roman god of war, was the time for military campaigns to begin again after a winter break. In the old Roman calendar, March was the first month of the year, when the sacred fire of Rome was renewed.

Summer was a time for fair-weather travel when days are longer and paths drier. The world we move through in spring and summer is denser, more tangly. But it is the best time to travel, even if woodland paths get overgrown. As I write this, I notice that many of these points are related to agricultural societies. What did spring and summer mean for Palaeolithic hunter-gatherers?

A change in the types, and abundance, of food in fair weather causes animal migrations and emergences from hibernation, which in turn requires different hunting and gathering strategies. For some in the past this would have meant increasing mobility, but it may have decreased it for others. In modern hunter-gatherer groups, spring and summer are often a time for childbirth, and for gathering and stockpiling supplies; a time of planning and preparation for times ahead, when the going might not be so good. We saw at the beginning of the book how the muddy ground of the Severn Estuary, marked with Mesolithic hunter-gatherer footprints, was dried and cracked by the summer heat. In the same vein, the 'footprint tuff' at Laetoli was peppered by tiny raindrops. Footmarks and weather marks.

As rivers and lakes freeze over in winter, a new type of mobility starts.[4] Bone skates from medieval and post-medieval London and York testify to the fun people must have had skating – or more accurately, sliding – over a frozen Thames or Ouse. Similar skates have been found elsewhere: Belgium and Holland, for example. These skates were generally made from the long, narrow shinbones of cattle and horses, often flattened on the bottom, having been worn down through use. They were attached to the bottom of shoes by a strip of leather that passed through holes in the skate and over the feet. Skaters propelled themselves by grasping a wooden pole with both hands and ramming its metal-tipped point into the ice between their legs, pulling and pushing themselves across the frozen surface.

When I was starting out in archaeology, I helped excavate many medieval bone skates from a site near Moorgate in the City of London, deep in the basement of an office block that was being replaced. After the Roman wall around Londinium was built, poor drainage caused the ground outside the wall in this area to become marshy. This waterlogging persisted throughout the Roman period and into the medieval. According to written accounts, during the cold winters of the late twelfth century, Moorfields, as it was known, froze over, furnishing a vast ice rink for medieval Londoners to skate on. The footwear I excavated was tangible archaeological evidence of their play.

Painful and awkward to wear as these skates may sound, experimental work in modern ice rinks has shown that they are surprisingly effective at gliding across the ice. Medieval chroniclers describe people travelling at high speeds, and even performing figures-of-eight. I love that experimental archaeologists attempted to recreate this activity. I fondly imagine them slipping and sliding, occasionally landing on their backsides, like the late Pleistocene hunter-gatherers at the cave of Tuc d'Audoubert in France.

*

For farming communities in particular, of course, the seasons have existential importance. And as we have seen, in both prehistoric and historic times, seasonal movements between uplands and lowlands, or wetlands and drylands, formed part of annual cycles. Later prehistoric societies built a number of monuments across Britain and Ireland to align with celestial events at certain times of the year. The most famous, Stonehenge, is aligned with the sunrise and sunset of the midsummer and midwinter solstice – the longest and shortest days of the year, when the sun appears to pause its movements as the year pivots and enters a new season (solstice, from the Latin *sol* and *stitium*: stilled sun). The same is true of Newgrange in Ireland and Maeshowe in the Orkneys, and the stone circles of Castlerigg and Long Meg and Her Daughters in Cumbria. The Thornborough henges in North Yorkshire even seem to reference Orion's Belt.

These monuments are an intertwining of skyscapes and landscapes. Summer and winter and rise and set – the movements of the sun and other celestial bodies are ever present, and built into monuments and peoples' lives.

We know that people looked to the heavens in pre-history. One of the world's oldest known depictions of the sky is the Nebra sky disc – a bronze disc with sheet-gold appliqués, a little over 30 centimetres in diameter and weighing in at around two kilograms. It was made, and used, in the Bronze Age, sometime around 1750–1550 BCE. The gold leaf forms the images of a series of celestial bodies: the sun or perhaps a full moon, as well as a crescent moon and stars, including the Pleiades constellation, which I know better as the Seven Sisters. The Pleiades are calendar stars – they mark the passing of the seasons since they disappear from the night sky in March and reappear in October. A grooved, curved object on the edge may be a rainbow, or perhaps a mythological barge that carried the sun at night – nocturnal counterpart to the sun horse we saw earlier. Gold strips on the sides of the disc mark the summer and winter solstices, so that the sky disc enshrines both astronomical and mythical knowledge.

This remarkable object had an unusual discovery. It was found on a warm summer's afternoon in 1999 by two illegal metal detectorists – just one object in a large hoard of swords, axes and armbands – on the Mittelberg hill near Nebra, Saxony-Anhalt in Germany. The artefacts were pulled from their resting place in the ground and conveyed, in the back of a Trabant owned by one of the men, to his home, where they were cleaned in his bathtub using washing-up liquid and wire wool. (Please do not follow this procedure if you find yourself cleaning an ancient artefact!) Their value was immediately clear and they were rapidly sold on. As news of the discovery spread, at first through detectorist groups, and then dealers and eventually museums, the hoard, including the sky disc, changed hands for ever greater sums of money. The objects eventually ended up with owners in Switzerland. News of the discovery made it to the newly appointed state archaeologist Dr Harald Meller – now a distinguished museum curator – in 2001, and a criminal investigation began.

In 2002 the sky disc was offered for sale again, this time to a museum, for a whopping €700,000. Dr Meller agreed to meet the seller in a hotel in Basel. In a scene more reminiscent of a John le Carré novel than archaeology, they met and as soon as the seller produced the bronzes – together with a contract for sale – Swiss police swooped in. The items were returned to Germany. The suspects made some desperate and eccentric claims – first that the sky disc had bewitched them, then that Dr Meller was completely mad – but were successfully prosecuted.[5]

So, the sky disc has certainly moved around a lot in recent times. But what I find much more interesting is that its manufacture embodies ancient movements. Not only does it depict the movement of heavenly bodies, encoding a calendar and revealing extensive astronomical knowledge, but the metalwork speaks of the small-scale movements of unknown craftspeople: the tiny tap, taps of hammer on gold sheet, the disc being turned around in the hand or placed on a small anvil stone before being rubbed by a probing thumb and held up to the eye for close inspection. At a larger scale the materials that made it had moved too. The copper had come from Salzburg in Austria, and some of the gold from Romania. The tin and the rest of the gold are likely to have come all the way from Cornwall. More than that even, isotope analysis points to a particular spot in Cornwall: the gold, it seems, was panned in the Carnon River, a river now spectacularly polluted with toxic water due to historic mining of metals.

*

Our modern world has done much to minimise the inconvenience of weather, the changing seasons, and their effect on our various landscapes, transforming human history in the process. But still today we are affected by the real world, with all its joys and dangers. No landscape is a blank slate, and mobility is never abstract. It always varies, and responding to that variety is a huge part of what it means to be human.

PART 5

Hero's journey

16. TIME'S MARCH:
CROSSING CONTINENTS

....

In which heroes journey and objects travel

....

The lure of the distant horizon is a powerful force, and it accounts for many of the world's greatest stories. In Greek myth, and much else since then, heroes have travelled far and wide before coming home wiser. Odysseus endured twenty years of adventures and returned in rags, a king in disguise. His tale, in its essentials, is not so different from the more recent adventures of the little hobbit Bilbo Baggins. Stories like these, describing what's been called 'the hero's journey', loom large in our consciousness – and it seems they always have.[1]

The past, too, is full of heroic travellers and their tales. People from all walks of life willingly travelled great distances

in medieval Europe. We have already met the pilgrims, travelling to any number of sacred shrines on the continent, as well as across seas to the Holy Land. This took on new levels during the Crusade years, which saw thousands of people, regardless of status, on the move; while the *peregrinatio perpetua* – pilgrims in endless travel – had no fixed earthly destination in their search for God. They wandered as a way of finding themselves. The very origin of the word *peregrinus* means 'foreigner': the pilgrim a perpetual stranger.

Merchants, of course, were in ceaseless motion, sometimes travelling very great distances to foreign lands – the Vikings, for example, who tapped into the networks of the Silk Roads, traversing modern Russia and into the Islamic world. Missionaries, high-level couriers, diplomats and ambassadors travelled far beyond Christendom.

The thirteenth-century Flemish Franciscan missionary William of Rubruck spent two years on the road to the court of the Great Khan at Karakorum, the capital of the Mongol empire. A few decades later, the Venetian merchant Marco Polo spent an impressive 24 years travelling across the Mongol empire, meeting Kublai Khan in present-day China, and visiting Persia, India, Japan and other parts of south and south-east Asia. Greatest of all travellers in the Middle Ages, though, was the Islamic scholar Ibn Battuta, who was on the road from 1325 to 1354, travelling across Europe, parts of Africa and much of Asia, even visiting the Maldive Islands, where he lived for a year and a half, taking, and then leaving behind, four wives and a number of concubines.

These travellers were often voyaging into the unknown, or at least the barely known. Their journeys, which were measured not in yards and miles but months and years, were physically hard, risky. Success – and even survival – was in no way guaranteed. Travel in antiquity often resulted in illness and disease. The very word 'travel' derives from the fourteenth-century word for toil or labour, now found in the word 'travail', meaning a painful or laborious effort. The long-distance traveller needed to make a will, or at least peace with the world.

By anyone's reckoning these were extraordinary undertakings. If they were successful, the rewards, both spiritual and economic, were high: dazzling jewels, pungent spices, glittering cloth and sensational tales.

One of the lures of travel is the possibility of freedom from social constraints, or the search for self-realisation. Another reason is to find love, or to follow a loved one. But curiosity is the human trait that has, above all, driven people to move very great distances. This may be to see what's around the next corner, or over the mountain. Or it may be the desire to understand foreign lives and customs.

This brings us to another reason people travelled great distances, a point made by the anthropologist Mary Helms: people travel in search of knowledge – the customs, songs, stories, crafts or sacred texts of foreign people. By gaining esoteric knowledge from distant lands, travellers can be accorded an aura of prestige and fame, and this can, and often is, used for political and religious gain.[2]

The wise stranger, or travelling craftsman, appears in many myths and stories. Think of Daedalus, who built wonders for mythical King Minos on Crete, including the labyrinth, and then flew away on wax wings. As we will see in the next chapter, travellers pass on crafts, including those as fundamental as farming and metallurgy. Many of the great innovations of prehistory were, I'm sure, the result of travel.

*

Objects brought back from a journey are felt to be strange and precious. They are marked by their foreignness – their exoticness – and are redolent of the journey itself.

Quite often the effort to acquire them adds to their potency and value, so that they can become symbolically charged. As Mary Helms points out, things from faraway places – precisely because they are exotic and rare – may be displayed in royal courts. A polar bear to a royal menagerie, for instance, or a rhinoceros given to a pope. Or they may become sacred, and used in ceremonies: frankincense and myrrh used as priestly oils and incense in the ancient Mediterranean world, to take another example.[3]

The instinct to collect esoteric knowledge and exotic objects is not exclusive to royal courts. Most of us share it. When I was nineteen and full of adventure, I left home to travel solo, driven by a yearning sense of wanderlust from a childhood of travel, and years of stifling school.

I cleaned planes at Gatwick airport for a summer, until I had earned enough money to travel in one of them. I taught English for five months at a small school in Nepal, for board and bedding, before heading off around India for the next six months. I travelled around the perimeter of this vast country, until I was back where I started. Stepping away from the familiar is often thrilling enough on its own, but here the chaos and richness, combined with the heat and dust, struck me with an intensity unthinkable at home. It animated me.

As far as I was concerned, I was trailblazing. Of course, I knew that I wasn't, having met legions of similarly attired – and privileged – gap-yearing youths. But this was *my* heroic journey.

Returning home almost a year later, and having left my teenage years behind, I discovered, as all travellers do, that the world I returned to was changed. It was also indifferent to the changes in me. I had climbed the foothills of the Himalayas and crossed deserts on a camel, I had cut my way through jungle and travelled the backwaters of Kerala by boat. But back at home, life continued much as it was. My family were pleased to see me, but not overwhelmingly impressed.

It's so easy, as archaeologists, to look for a generalised understanding of people in the past, because we don't really 'see' the individual. But each individual really did experience their own life differently – as a kind of 'hero's journey', no matter how modest – and I try to remind myself of that. I carried my journey with me in tales that got taller with each insufferable retelling. I took my own equivalent of an exotic rhinoceros through my university years, in the form of colourful, baggy cotton trousers and sandals, until a particularly harsh Welsh winter forced me to put on socks and shoes.

*

In the archaeological record we find that people have gone to great lengths to collect, mine or quarry materials from a particular source, and carry them over great distances. Often these places are themselves important, but the journey is too. The value and power of the material is related to the value of the journey.[4]

Archaeology records many examples of potent or valuable objects that have travelled long distances. The Neolithic polished jade axe-head we saw earlier alongside the Sweet Track in Somerset was one. Many more of these jade axe-heads have been found across Britain and Europe, and we can trace something of their journeys. A new technique of analysis, borrowed from space exploration, measures the rock's mineral composition by the way it absorbs light of particular wavelengths, so that, amazingly, the precise source of the stone can be identified, often right down to the specific outcrop. This shows that the jade derived from the Italian Alps: Monte Viso, south-west of Turin, and Monte Beigua above Genoa. The makers would have had to climb to heights of over 2,000 metres to extract this rare rock. The quarried blocks were first roughed out into an axe-head shape by hitting flakes off and gently pecking with a hammer-stone, and then, over many laborious hours, they were ground and polished to give them a luminous green and glassy sheen. These were precious ceremonial objects rather than everyday tools. Similar processes can be seen with the ground and polished greenstone axe-heads that were quarried in Cumbria in northern England during the Neolithic and distributed across Britain and Ireland. The stone was selected and quarried from the area of Great Langdale in the Lake District, particularly a high and quite inaccessible outcrop known as the Pike of Stickle. The not inconsiderable effort required to climb to the outcrop and then quarry the material was symbolically important, rather than just a functional consideration.

These hard-won pieces sometimes travelled long distances – for the jade axe-heads that could be as much as 1,800 km from their source – passing through many hands, being reshaped and repolished along their journey. Each axe-head had its own story; its own biography. 'Green treasures from faraway, magic mountains,' as Alison Sheridan, one of the archaeologists involved in their study, nicely put it in a talk I heard recently. And these prized pieces of place became cherished heirlooms, since they circulated over centuries, being passed down through the generations, before being deposited in the ground, often after being deliberately broken.[5]

I realised this when I was excavating at Marden henge. In one corner of the huge monument, a broken piece of Cumbrian greenstone axe-head was unearthed. This had been made probably a thousand years before the henge, and had been circulating through most of the Neolithic period. In its broken and fragmentary state, it had somehow come to be deposited in the henge. An offering perhaps, or a way of controlling its power. The axe-head was redolent of the journeys it had taken, each breakage and knock adding to its biography. It told a story; probably many stories – all of them now lost to us.

Elsewhere, people from aboriginal groups in Australia travel, or trade, over long distances to obtain stone or ochre even though similar material is available locally. It is made symbolically more powerful by the journey.[6] Movement provides meaning that is written into the objects. As they are circulated and exchanged, they move further from their original source. They become caught up in their own networks of travel, drifting between and across the flows of people as they are bartered, given as gifts, stolen or lost and found.[7] They represent obligations and dependencies, and become markers of connections between people as they pass through different sets of hands. They remain in some places longer than others – sitting on shelves, or dormant in museum cabinets, or lost and buried in the ground, only to be dug up again, like the Nebra sky disc, and recirculated with an even richer story attached to them.

Mobility can be transformational for things as much as it is for people. But objects can also gather people and pull them in. Think of a famous artwork, a Van Gogh or Cézanne, and the power it has to draw people to see it. On a bigger scale, a site like Stonehenge does the same. Similarly, we've seen how folk travelled very great distances in the medieval world to see particular saints' relics in cathedrals and monasteries. They were potent objects with the power to mobilise.[8]

Passing through time as well as space, these things become repositories for collective and intergenerational memories, heirlooms travelling along paths of descent. They become ancestral items, artefacts of memory that have the power to slow down history.[9] Looking back, we find our way into the past by the objects dropped, like Hansel and Gretel following a trail of pebbles in the forest.

17. ONE WAY: ROUTES AND ROOTS

In which we see that migration made our world, and continues to do so

Three decades before I went on my heroic journey, wanderlust had brought my mother and father together.

My dad was an aircraft engineer, at first with the RAF and later with a commercial airline. My mum was originally a nurse at Guy's Hospital in London, but felt constrained by its austere world and rebelled, seeking freedom in the high life as an air hostess. The 1960s were the glamour days of flying, a new form of commercial mobility that brought the world closer together.

My mother and father worked on the same planes – the hostess and the 'flying spanner', as flight engineers were known. They saw the world together, often operating the 'Hajj flight' from Afghanistan to Saudi Arabia for access to Mecca.

Skyfaring sweethearts on their own pilgrimage of love, they married and had a family (me the middle of three) and remained peripatetic, living in Malaysia, Fiji, then Cyprus – airborne children in tow – and later India,

Hong Kong and China. De-placed perhaps, but never not 'at home'.

Too early, but after a life well lived, my mother has gone, and my father, now in his eighties, has settled in Spain. I treat the word 'settled' in the loosest possible sense, though, for although his American road trip days are probably behind him, his compulsion to travel is vast. It is, I am sure, a form of dromomania (from the Greek *dromos*: 'running' or 'racetrack').

*

Not all travel is in both directions. Not everyone comes back.

The *Mayflower* pilgrims settled for ever in the American colonies, as did millions upon millions of European migrants who followed them over several centuries, by ocean liner and then by plane. They may have looked back, but they didn't return.

That kind of movement is not always a privilege. Legions of enslaved Africans taken to work on plantations in the Americas did not return home. Like them, criminals were transported against their will from Britain to America, then – following the Declaration of Independence – to Australia. So too were orphaned and destitute British and Irish children, sent to become indentured servants.

And these migrations, both willing and unwilling, dispossessed communities that had been rooted in those soils for thousands of years.

Global migration increased throughout the nineteenth and twentieth centuries, reaching a colossal scale in the years after the Second World War. People fled their homes as a result of human rights abuses or found themselves displaced as the boundaries in Eastern Europe were redrawn. Others moved in desperate hope of opportunities to make a living.

From 1945 to the 1960s, tens of thousands of people migrated to Britain from Ireland, from across Eastern Europe, Italy, Malta, Cyprus, and from India, Pakistan and the Caribbean. Many were encouraged to work in essential industries, from mining and textiles to hospitals – as doctors and nurses, or, more commonly, as porters, stokers and cleaners. At the same time large numbers of people left Britain, bunched into boats sailing from Southampton and Liverpool, headed for a new life in Australia, New Zealand and Canada. To these migrations we can add Russians to Siberia, Dutch to South Africa, and Chinese to Taiwan.[1]

In summary, migration created our modern world, and continues to shape it. The news is full of people migrating, whether fleeing something terrible (starvation, persecution, war, poverty, climate change), drawn to something attractive (better pay and prospects, to fill skills shortages, or a generalised dream of a better life), or both.

Less well understood is that migration created the ancient world too. This process has always been going on, at different rates in different places and times.

There's a German word, *Völkerwanderung* – the wandering of the peoples – used to describe the migration period in Europe in the first millennium of the Common Era. There were the movements of Langobards into Italy, and Avars into the Hungarian plain. Vikings left Scandinavia for Greenland, and Germanic-speaking groups in the fifth and sixth centuries CE crossed the North Sea to southern and eastern Britain to create what must have been a wonderfully diverse population speaking a variety of languages. Early medieval sources, such as the writing of the sixth-century monk Gildas, Bede's eighth-century *Ecclesiastical History of the English People* or the ninth-century *Anglo-Saxon Chronicle* testify to the Angles, Saxons and Jutes arriving in Britain.

Earlier still, the ethnically diverse Roman empire was created by considerable movement and migration. The empire extended from Hadrian's Wall to North Africa, from the Rhine to the Euphrates, and it is unsurprising that people travelled widely across it. They were, in fact, encouraged to do so. Soldiers were recruited from, and posted to, all parts of the empire, many eventually marrying, settling and raising families there. Administrators, merchants, women and children moved around and created new lives for themselves away from their natal homes. We know from written accounts and graveside inscriptions that soldiers from Ethiopia and Syria were garrisoned on Hadrian's Wall, and major towns were melting pots of people from the Mediterranean and beyond. The evidence from archaeology – inscriptions, burial goods, and the remains of the people themselves – overwhelmingly attest to this diversity and movement.

And before that? In the vast expanse of prehistory, people travelled constantly, settling far and wide. Waves of early migrations show the genus *Homo* moving within Africa and into Eurasia over millions of years. This includes members of our own species, *Homo sapiens*, who began to travel out of Africa probably less than 100,000 years ago, following routes pursued by our human relatives, of the species *Homo erectus*, across the world 2 million years ago.[2]

The tracks of these movements leave distinctive genetic signatures, although continuous stirring and mixing mean that they are not always easy to read. This is a field of study known as archaeogenetics, and there have been spectacular breakthroughs in the extraction and sequencing of ancient DNA recently that, like the isotope analyses we saw earlier, have challenged and changed archaeological interpretations of the past.

Each one of us contains in our genome information about a host of ancestors: an entire population history. By studying this, archaeogeneticists can establish the genetic make-up of the ancestral population, and see influxes of groups of people with different ancestral histories. What they are finding is that the mixture between highly different populations is a recurrent feature of humanity.[3] Combined with archaeology, comparative linguistics and the study of isotopes, archaeogenetics is revolutionising how we study, and what we know about, past movements.

The greatest impact so far has been on our understanding of later prehistory, where archaeogeneticists have identified a series of epochal waves of migration in Europe; waves that largely displaced local populations. This is a fast-moving area of science and summaries go out of date before they can be published. (As I write, the discovery of a new wave of prehistoric migration has just been announced, this time in the Middle to Late Bronze

Age, around the same time as the wheel and the horse were introduced to Britain. I hear that further discoveries are imminent for later periods too!) I will focus on two migration events: one at the beginning of the Bronze Age, and an earlier wave at the start of the Neolithic.

The later of the two is the Early Bronze Age culture known for its distinctive-looking Beaker pottery, which resembles an upside-down bell. These pots were decorated by pressing cord into the soft clay before firing to create patterns. They're very elegant. I have a replica on my mantelpiece. To me, it looks modern and the aesthetic is quite beautiful.

The Beaker culture is recorded across continental Europe. It arrived in Britain a little after 2500 BCE, and marks a very distinct change in the archaeological record from the preceding Neolithic period. In fact, the Beaker period represents a horizon between the Stone Age and the Bronze Age. It's when we see, for the first time, metals in the form of gold and copper (bronze developed slightly later). It also indicates a change in the way people buried their dead, away from cremations and towards individual graves under round barrows (mounds). This hints at a deeper change in culture, and in the way the world – and perhaps the afterlife – was understood.

So: we have known for a long time that this period marked an important change, but we didn't know how it came about. Was it the spread of people, or only of their ideas and prestige objects?

The study of ancient DNA (aDNA) has demonstrated unambiguously that the Beaker culture was introduced into Britain by people who were descended from populations originating from the Eurasian steppe – the same place where we saw the development of horse-riding. In Britain there is no evidence of steppe ancestry in ancient DNA until the Bronze Age. Afterwards, there's plenty.

The evidence is overwhelming: a tremendous wave of immigration into Late Neolithic Britain from the east resulted in a large genetic turnover, suggesting a substantial influx of new people. The genetic and archaeological impact was dramatic and permanent.[4]

*

One person from the past, more than any other, shows us something of this movement.

First, picture this scene: 2002 and the Friday before the early May bank holiday weekend in the small town of Amesbury in Wiltshire, five kilometres south-east of Stonehenge. Archaeologists, on hands and knees and using trowels, scrape clean a patch of ground that has already been reduced down by the bucket of a mechanical digger. They examine the surface with their expert eyes for archaeological features, before a planned new primary school is constructed. It is already known that this patch of land is peppered with important archaeology, not least two Roman cemeteries. One of these cemeteries had been excavated before they started work, and the other isn't going to be damaged by the development and so will be left in the ground. The archaeologists can see two slightly unusual features, three metres apart from one another, in the area of the new school. Probably Roman graves: outliers from one of the cemeteries perhaps, but they need to be excavated otherwise they'll be destroyed. A relatively easy job then – just two Roman graves – for a Friday, which is, after all, POETS day ('Piss off early, tomorrow's Saturday'). Plenty of time to excavate and record them before knocking off for the long weekend. Except that didn't happen, because these weren't run-of-the-mill Roman graves. They weren't even Roman. They turned out to be two of the most important Bronze Age Beaker burials in Europe.

When the importance of these graves was clear, the archaeologists, under the management of Andrew Fitzpatrick, did not leave the site until every scrap of archaeology had been bagged, tagged and recorded. It was too important to leave half done, especially over a bank holiday weekend; and in addition some passers-by had already heard the news that gold had been found – news travels fast, especially along paths. The archaeologists worked through the day and then deep into the night, using torches and car headlights. They finally finished at 2am.

From this excavation – and the sterling work of the archaeologists – we now know more about this important period of transition, and we can tell the story of the graves. The richer of the two was once lined with wood to form a mortuary chamber below ground, although the wood had rotted away. It once had a covering mound, but that had been long since scoured away. Within the chamber was the well-preserved skeleton of a man aged between 35 and 45 years old. He was buried lying on his left side with his knees pulled up in a foetal position. His right arm was bent and touching the opposing shoulder. Around him – on his person and laid out in his chamber – was a large collection of objects, making it the most richly furnished Bronze Age burial ever found in Britain. It included things that he might need in the afterlife, like a collection of flint and antler tools, the latter possibly for flint-knapping, a beautifully made antler cloak pin, as well as a strike-a-light kit for making a fire. He had three copper knives, and around him were five ceramic Beaker pots.[5]

On his forearm was a stone wristguard, sometimes known as a bracer; protection worn by an archer against the recoil of a bowstring. A spare wristguard lay nearby, and around him were seventeen delicate and beautifully made barbed and tanged flint arrowheads; the wooden shafts they had been originally attached to were no longer present. These arrows may have been thrown into his grave like flowers at a funeral, as the artist Jane Brayne evocatively put it in her wonderful comic book about the site. The presence of archery gear meant that he was immediately named the Amesbury Archer.

He probably was an archer, too, since analysis of his bones showed similar changes to his skeleton as the archers from the *Mary Rose*. This analysis also showed he was missing his left kneecap, the result of a traumatic injury that would have left him with a significant disability, and probably unable to straighten his left leg.

To me, and to many archaeologists, though, the greater importance was the evidence of metalworking. Behind him in his grave, he had a little black polished cushion stone, which would have been used as a portable anvil for beating copper and gold sheet. In front of him he had two tiny pieces of curled gold in the shape of little baskets.

They are thought to be earrings or hair tresses, or perhaps ornaments from an item of clothing. I have already mentioned the copper knives, and he also had four boar's tusks, which are thought to be involved in metalworking somehow, perhaps to smooth and burnish metal objects.

Dating to between 2380 and 2290 BCE, soon after the huge lintelled sarsen stones at Stonehenge were going up, the Amesbury Archer is one of the very first of the new wave of metalworkers in Britain. The copper knives and gold ornaments are among the oldest known pieces of worked metal in the country. To me, he should be known as the Amesbury Metalworker, although I admit that has less of an alliterative ring about it. But these items mark him out as a craftsman, as much as the other bits mark him as an archer. And of course, his rich grave means he was a man of status. Part of an elite.

I mentioned that there were two graves. This other one contained a Bronze Age burial too, but not nearly as richly furnished. This burial was of another man, younger, perhaps in his late twenties. He died a generation or two after the Archer, and aDNA shows that they were not closely related; at most they were cousins, or possibly great-grandfather and great-grandson. He too had a pair of gold basket earrings or hair tresses (the jury's still out on what these actually are), as well as a boar's tusk, which, as we've seen, may be related to metalworking (the jury's out on this too).

A year after the work on the Amesbury Archer and his companion, archaeologists working in advance of a new water pipe uncovered another exceptional burial, less than a kilometre away at a place called Boscombe

Down. Again, the pit had been lined with wood to form a burial chamber, but instead of just one individual it contained the remains of nine people: one articulated adult man, surrounded by the disarticulated remains of other people of a variety of ages, from adult, to juvenile, to an infant. With the burials were eight beakers and a series of arrowheads. No gold this time, but the arrowheads did earn the occupants the pleasingly alliterative name of the Boscombe Bowmen. It has been interpreted as something akin to a family vault, and the remains were seemingly put in over a period of time. The earliest date to between 2500 and 2340 BCE, so likely earlier than the Amesbury Archer. The last died between 2330 and 2200 BCE.

There is another part to this story, though. We saw earlier in the book how isotopic signatures in your food and drink fix in your tooth enamel and elsewhere in your skeleton. These analyses have been applied to the Amesbury Archer, his companion and the Boscombe Bowmen. The oxygen isotopes for the Archer's premolars, which formed in early childhood, and his third molars, which formed in early adolescence, provided the same result, showing that he grew up in continental Europe, in the regions around the western Alps, an area in which metalworking was well established by this time. And analysis of his aDNA confirms that his paternal-line ancestry derived from steppe pastoralists. He was a migrant. The isotope results from his companion were different, his second premolar indicating he was born on the Wessex chalk downs, but analysis of his third molar shows something quite remarkable: it suggests that when he was between nine and thirteen years old, he was living outside Britain, quite possibly in the same region where the Archer grew up. Although he was born and died in the Wessex countryside, he still had ties to his ancestral land, and spent at least some of his childhood there, perhaps being fostered by relatives. This reminds us that movement is complex and multidirectional.

The results for the Bowmen were less clear. Many seem to have started life somewhere that wasn't Wessex, but could have been elsewhere in Britain or Ireland, or even continental Europe. The first individuals to be buried may well have come from Wales or Cumbria. The finds and nature of the burial, and the early date of it, suggest a continental link as well, though.

Here we have the story of the start of the Bronze Age. Of course, it is the story as told by just a few, and, in reality, it will have varied from region to region. But the Amesbury Archer and his neighbours neatly encapsulate the story that is developing out of archaeogenetics. He most likely grew up in the Alps. He then travelled, perhaps north along the valley of the River Rhine and over the Channel to Britain, or – more likely – west, across France, to the Atlantic coast. He presumably sailed in a hide boat, or maybe an early form of the sewn-plank boat (of which we'll hear more shortly). As is so often the case, we know the start and end, but not the journey in between. We don't know when he got his devastating knee injury, but he may have made this journey as a disabled man. What, I wonder, must that have been like for him?

He really was a traveller, and of some distance, cross-ing land and sea. A metalworker; a travelling craftsman. The Daedalus of his time. And he had privileged access to this knowledge. This will have given him status. The materials he carried with him had travelled too, since they were from a variety of places. The copper for his knives, for instance, was from both Iberia and France, while the cushion stone, and one of his wristguards, derived from somewhere in continental Europe. Some of the gold also came from the continent, the rest from Cornwall. What value was placed on these objects? What biographies did they have, and what journeys had they been on?

These people were part of a new wave, unrelated to the preceding Neolithic. Their ancestry, and their links, were eastwards to the steppe. They had different mate-rials and technologies, and distinct styles of pottery, and they did things in disparate ways.

*

I remarked that archaeogeneticists have identified an earlier wave of migration. This involved the arrival of Neolithic people – the people whose DNA was itself largely replaced, later, by the likes of the Amesbury Archer.

Once again, archaeology has long shown a clear divi-sion between the hunter-gatherers of the Mesolithic and the Neolithic farmers who came after. We see no animal or plant domestication in the Mesolithic period, and no significant construction of monuments. But after around 4000 BCE we find in Britain cereal production, ploughing and dairying. Neolithic Britons transformed landscapes and constructed sometimes huge monuments. The archaeological evidence is clear – again – but until recently we could not be sure if this was merely a diffusion of ideas and objects, or the movement of people themselves. Battles raged for decades among archaeologists who fervently believed one theory or other, and conferences on the subject have ended as all-out shouting matches.

Again, aDNA changes everything. The evidence is unequivocal. The two populations of the Mesolithic and Neolithic are genetically different. The Mesolithic population derived from groups who had expanded across Europe after the last glacial period (termed Western Hunter-gatherers), while the Neolithic population in Britain arrived with genetic ancestry from Anatolia (modern-day Turkey) and the Near East. It wasn't just ideas and objects that travelled: it was people, and in significant numbers.

They moved on foot and in boats. They brought ideas and different ways of doing things, and they settled in foreign lands with cereals and livestock. Their movements changed the genetic make-up – and the history – of Europe.[6]

By the end of the Neolithic in Britain, the Western Hunter-gatherer ancestry had all but disappeared, replaced by the people descended from those deriving from Anatolia.

What this means is that none of us can really claim as our ancestors the people of the Mesolithic or Neolithic. No one can say that we are related to the builders of Stonehenge. It shows the absurdity of ancestral 'purity'. Genetically speaking, there is no such thing as race. It is an illusion, a story we've told ourselves so we can believe that our place and identity are intimately connected and shouldn't change.

That is not to deny social and cultural groups and distinctions among populations, because these differences and diversities can be important too. But just imagine how many migrations have occurred over the course of human history and prehistory since those footprints were planted in Tanzania 3.5 million years ago.

There's every reason to believe that population changes like the ones just described occurred throughout prehistory, deep into the Palaeolithic, across almost unimaginable timescales, with successive waves of migrations out of Africa.

People have always moved and settled into new areas, filling niches across the globe.

Some of those migrations were hugely significant, as we've seen: altering and introducing genes, as well as language, innovation, technology, art, religion and material culture. Most were minor – hugely significant to the individuals involved, no doubt, but having little impact on the population as a whole, or the archaeological record. Taken together, aDNA and archaeology demonstrate that humankind has flowed out constantly, in all directions, twisting and turning to form a rhizomatic, entangled mesh of genes and cultural diversity.

The very patterning of human existence and diversity has only come about through millennia of people moving and mixing. Everyone is an outsider, descendant of outsiders, and our own descendants will almost certainly be the same. We are all immigrants. The gene pool is always being stirred, mixed and overlaid – because we have always been restless.

*

The findings based on aDNA settle many questions, but open up new ones. Such as: what kind of migrations brought agriculture to Britain and (later) the Beaker culture? Were they small- or large-scale population movements? Did they come in groups or as scattered individuals? Were they free adventurers, indentured migrants or refugees? Expelled, exiled or émigrés?

Lacking a written record, we can't answer definitively. But the migrations of the Bronze Age that we have just seen weren't necessarily violent. In fact, the clues point the opposite way, to high levels of female as well as male migration. So, no invading warrior bands, no sense of societies being squashed or wiped out. Wanderers, not invaders. Many archaeological sites and monuments continued to be used despite the changes. Perhaps the people with steppe ancestry infilled less inhabited areas first, expanding only gradually, over many generations. There is also evidence for plague pathogens at this time, and archaeogeneticists have suggested that steppe people may have brought with them an epidemic that, not unlike that of the conquistadors in South America, depopulated landscapes, allowing for greater expansion. Like ideas, innovations and objects, whenever people move, diseases do too.

And the Neolithic? Also no charging horde of invading immigrants, but more of a slow diaspora, expanding into new areas over many generations, over thousands of years. At certain times and places, we do find archaeological evidence for violence, but in other places it seems to have been more peaceful – an infilling of vacant space.

We don't know all the answers, but we can acknowledge the difficulty behind the questions. Migration, like any form of mobility, is complex and entangled, and does not follow a single recipe. Migrants are not all the same; they come from different backgrounds and have different skills and resources. As we've seen, the motive can be a mixture of push and pull. On top of that, the decision actually to migrate – instead of just talking about it – and the specific paths people take, may vary according to age, gender, marital status and whether or not they have children.

Similarly, the speed at which people move varies. Those escaping conflict or persecution may move quickly and desperately, while other communities have time and choices and may trickle into a new area over time, perhaps returning home to collect family.

As archaeologists and historians, we are often obliged to try to make sense of this complexity while also remembering that the facts may hardly fit even our most 'rational' explanations.

For instance: the decision to migrate – to uproot from one's native soil and depart for an entirely unfamiliar geographic and cultural location – seems, when we look at it with the benefit of hindsight, to be different from the other travels we have seen in this book. It looks like a deliberate decision to make a new life, cutting off the past to become a 'foreigner', an outsider who belongs neither here nor there. But that may not always have been the original intention. Many who migrated may have intended to return home.[7]

If they did, they returned as outsiders who, by missing out on much of everyday life and special events, might never properly fit back in. And fitting in – or not – is one of the great difficulties of migration. It's natural to want to belong.

But differences can inspire fear, depending on where migrants come from, their economic status, the language they speak, food they eat and clothes they wear. People fear that migrants will bring strange illnesses, steal things, take jobs. Anti-immigrant sentiments and politics are politically charged topics right now, with migrating people depicted by hostile observers as less than human – barely more than animals or zombies, 'invading' in 'hordes'. Similar sentiments can be found throughout written history, and presumably before that.[8]

At best, migration is a transformative, creative process for all concerned, a cultural mixing that diversifies life and culture in all its forms: art, music, literature, language, cuisine, genes, ideas. And this benefits the wider community. Life becomes creolised and hybridised. It becomes a little more mobile.[9]

It is transformative not only for the displaced person, but for the people around them too. Everyone becomes a bit 'elsewhere'. And while migration sets people apart and shows up differences, it also provides an opportunity for solidarity, bringing people and communities together. When that happens, the displaced person can embrace his or her outsider status, their 'foreignness'. They can make something of their roots and their routes – the places they come from, and their voyage out.

In the past, the journey to a new land, which bonded the people who travelled together, and provided an opportunity to learn about themselves and others, gradually became idealised. But that's because, as we shall see, they really were heroes' journeys.

18. SEAFARING: ACROSS OCEANS OF TIME

In which we glimpse the wild and furious history of ocean crossings, and say farewell as our journey together comes to an end

Near the village of Holme-next-the-Sea in Norfolk, where earth, sea and sky meet, a local man called John Lorimer was out beachcombing in the spring of 1998. He spotted something he'd not seen before: pieces of wood sticking out of silts that had been exposed by recent sea erosion.

He came back again, and again. And after carefully observing the exposed wood over a number of visits, he contacted the Castle Museum in Norwich. They sent somebody down to take a look. Initially, investigators concluded that it was the remains of a medieval fish trap. But how to explain a 4,000-year-old bronze axe-head that was found there? Whatever it was, the site was older than medieval – much, much older.

Working carefully, the archaeologists gradually came to realise that it was, in fact, an extraordinarily well-preserved – but fragile – Bronze Age timber circle.

Because it was rapidly eroding, English Heritage agreed to fund a complete excavation to remove this treasure. That was never going to be easy, because in a tidal zone you have only a few hours each day in which to excavate, and much of that time is spent bailing and sponging up water before any proper archaeological work can start.

This particular site had the added pressure of locals and neo-pagans protesting against the excavation, at one point even occupying the site. They protested because they did not want it removed from its assumed sacred location. But the choice was clear: remove it or lose it, for the erosive effects of the sea could not be stopped.

The excavation came to the attention of archaeology journals, then national newspapers, and the circle was soon dubbed Seahenge. Like Stonehenge, from which its name is taken, it is not a henge at all (you will remember that a henge is an earthen enclosure with a ditch on the inside of a bank), but an elliptical ring of 55 closely fitted oak posts, many carefully split in half, creating a space of around seven metres in diameter at the widest point. The posts themselves would have once stood three metres high. In the middle of this towering ring – this 'monster's toothy yawn' as I heard the archaeologist and artist Rose Ferraby describe it on the radio the other day – was the stump of a large oak tree, weighing some two and a half tons. Ropes of woven honeysuckle had been used to haul it into position. Curiously, the stump had been placed upside down, so that the trunk, which had been stripped of bark, disappeared into the ground and the roots spread out above it like a miniature canopy. A transposal of the natural order.

Dendrochronology (the science of tree-ring dating) tells us that the oaks were all felled in the same year: specifically, the spring and summer of 2049 BCE, at the start of the Bronze Age. We know the construction was a communal act because axe strokes, still visible on the timbers, demonstrate that at least 51 different axes were used in felling, splitting and modifying the oaks. So at least that number of people must have been involved – likely many more. A second timber circle was revealed nearby. This is of a similar date, but remains unexcavated.[1]

These monuments are hard to understand. But to me they suggest, as well as an inversion of the natural world, some kind of celebration. Celebration of what? Well, they were built on an area that was, at the time, saltmarsh. This was close to the point of the highest spring tides, tides caused by greater gravitational pull – the liminal zone, the border between land and sea.

*

The sea, and movement across it, has shaped the world we know. It has driven us to do remarkable things, and we have lived around it and on its islands, played in its shallows and on the sea shores, plundered it and fought on it, and crossed and re-crossed it countless times. It runs through us. It is wild and disordered, but we have made it central to our lives so that it represents vast corridors of connectivity. The sea is true mobility.

Written history is full of stories about this. In the tenth and ninth centuries BCE, the Phoenicians built complex ships and traded purple murex dye between Mogador and Tyre. Later, the Romans built a vast empire thanks to a navy that allowed them to invade distant lands and traffic huge quantities of foodstuffs – grain, wine, olive oil, salted fish and fish sauce known as *garum* – to feed that growing empire.

At the end of the Roman empire, existing systems of connectivity collapsed, and new ones developed. Large rowing vessels were probably common in the North Sea during this time, while Frisians, sailing in convoys, traded in luxury goods and ingots of copper alloy.

The best-known seafarers in Europe were the Norsemen and women whose traditional homeland was the maritime regions of Scandinavia. They had been trading and sailing widely for generations before the second half of the eighth century CE, when – in a period of astonishing mobility – they began travelling further afield: east along the Silk Roads and west to Britain and Ireland, Greenland and, long before Columbus, what would later be called North America.

Viking great ships, with single square sails of woven wool, could be moved by teams of rowers using sheer brute force. In these boats, they looked for people to trade with using skins, furs and walrus ivory, and luxury items such as amber from the eastern Baltic. Often travelling as families – men, women and children – they could spend months or sometimes years abroad establishing trade and communication networks and setting up encampments and commercial centres. Violence was a part of their life, as it was for most at the time, and they also raided, laying waste to land and holy places, killing some they met and enslaving others. But the Vikings emerging from both archaeology and a closer reading of history are far from the angry, rampaging barbarians of popular culture. Instead, they were merchants, diplomats and settlers, weaving intricate networks of trade and exploration from Russia and Turkey in the east to Canada in the west. We can see this in the archaeological record, from fragments of Chinese silk to carnelian beads from India, or in silver coins from the areas of modern-day Baghdad and St Petersburg. We can also see it in the trading centres they established that grew and thrived and attracted skilled craftsmen, from Dublin in Ireland to York in England, from Novgorod in Russia to Kyiv in Ukraine.[2]

The same kinds of maritime activity have continued to shape the world in the centuries after the Vikings, from wars to pilgrimages, from merchant adventurers to pirates, privateers and slave-traders. And inevitably, this busyness turned the seas into highways for information, for the exchange of news and intelligence. The Roman world had a well-established postal system, which included post-boats, so that news of the death of Gaius Caesar on the south coast of Anatolia in 4 CE was able to reach Pisa only 40 days later. In 1760 the news that King George II had died took six weeks to cross the Atlantic Ocean to reach colonial America. A few years later, details and updates on the American War of Independence made the same journey in the opposite direction to waiting London newspapers. By 1865, news of President Lincoln's assassination appeared in the British newspapers just twelve days after it happened.[3]

*

The open sea is the realm of the unbound and unrestricted. It pulls us to it and pushes us away, an ebb and flow of freedom and danger. It is a place of incalculable power, inspiring admiration and fear in equal parts. To travel across this briny expanse, even when others have done it before you, is to take a vast risk, because moving over water leaves no trace or path to follow. How many generations did it take, we might wonder, to assemble even a rudimentary understanding of navigation?

Just as a wayfarer intimately knows the land, seafarers learn to understand the meaning of the colour of the water, the way light reflects on it or sound bounces off it. They read the paths of seabirds, the waves and swell, predict currents and tides, in the same way a wayfarer reads animal prints, vegetation and topography. They navigate by looking at celestial bodies, and understand weather by being attuned to wind and cloud formations. They know the seasons – when winds of one kind will blow, while others will not. And to bring a vessel to shore they need knowledge of coastal forms and shifting sandbanks. If they want to survive, a traveller of the sea needs to have a *feel* for it. How many people died, learning those lessons?

It was not just an understanding of the practicalities, either, but of the rituals and cosmologies that surrounded going to sea, of which there are many. Throughout history, the people who learnt – and dared – to travel the seas acquired a particular identity. They were different from people who moved only on land. We see this in the artefacts left behind, from the Mesolithic to the modern day, the harpoons and leisters, the nets and hooks-and-line, and the boats themselves; the tangible evidence of an expression of a specific group's social identity. Still today, sailors like to make clear their difference, as they always have, whether by tattoos, special clothing, language, song, and so on. Their daily rhythms are different, governed not by day and night but by tide times or the movements of shoals of fish. Seafarers of all kinds, from prehistoric travellers to medieval fishermen, Viking explorers and nineteenth-century whalers, had distinct identities that drew together the crew for their shared travels, and the stories that grew out of them.[4]

But even to those familiar with it, the sea remains of course a place of profound danger and uncontrolled force, treacherous and capricious. Everything about this wilderness screams that you should not be out there. It's hardly surprising that many cultures believe that the world of the dead lies on the other side of water. With the possible exception of space travel, no other setting for human life has proved quite as challenging as the ocean, and a successful crossing is a transcendent achievement.

Something of this sacred quality is conveyed by legends and biblical stories – Jonah somehow surviving being swallowed by a whale, Jesus calming a storm. Inspired by these stories and others like them, a variety of holy men took to the seas in distant times, to test themselves in a watery wilderness, or to spread the word. They set off in small boats and put their faith in the hands of their god. For the *peregrini* – the travelling monks – the sea was a place to wander, seeking self-knowledge and salvation. It was their desert.[5] One who did that was the Irish monk Columba, who eventually settled on the little Hebridean island of Iona, sacred and secluded, in 563 CE, to establish a monastery.

In doing so, perhaps he acknowledged that the sea-shore marks the boundary between the known and the unknown that needs to be crossed.

*

Associations with the sea can be profound. Boats symbolise the sea, as well as the journey across it, giving them a significance far beyond mere functional use. We've seen how a horse draws the sun across the sky, but we've also heard how in some stories it is pulled through the underworld by a boat at night. In fact, boats were often seen as living things by those who used them. They were attributed agency, taking on the knowledge and experience of the journeys they had made.

We see something of this, as early as the beginning of the Iron Age in Britain, in little wooden objects known as the Roos Carr figures. These five naked, prehistoric models were found in 1836 about two metres below the ground by labourers digging a ditch near Withernsea in Holderness, East Yorkshire. Dating to around 600 BCE, they are carved from yew, and between 35 and 41 centimetres tall. Roughly hewn, like pieces of folk art, they may well represent warriors since they are armed, and have very angry, piercing, white quartzite eyes. Not unlike the eyes of a goshawk; eyes that let you know that they are the predator and you the prey. They also have huge, dangling penises, which are detachable, fitting into a carefully prepared slot in the figures' groins. (You can turn them so they don't dangle downwards but point skywards – excited warriors! Or pull them off completely to leave a hole, making the figures wonderfully gender-fluid.) Their arms are detachable as well, with little pegs at the end to fit into holes. To respect Victorian sensibilities, when the figures were originally displayed at the Hull Literary and Philosophical Society, soon after their discovery, the penises were removed from the groins and either put away for safekeeping, or, for the figures missing arms, slotted into the arm holes.

As well as the figures, the ditch-diggers found a wooden model of a boat. Just 56 centimetres long, it has a carved serpent's head that likewise once had white quartz eyes, not dissimilar to the Viking dragon-headed warships that would terrorise the same shores a thousand years later. Holes inside the boat show that the four warriors would have been standing in it, their peg-like legs slotting into the holes. The fifth model person was presumably part of a different crew and boat: we assume that more figures remain in the ground. Deposited into a watery context, the whole thing probably represents a votive offering, perhaps to help with safe passage for sailors. But what I want to emphasise is that the boat is zoomorphic; it is depicted as a living creature. This is typical of boats. Around the world, sailors give names and identities to their boats and put figureheads on them. They animate them. They are more than functional objects; more than conveyances. After all, the sailors' lives depend on them.

At many times, and in many parts of the world, boats have been buried with the dead, or incorporated into funerary rites, perhaps to help the deceased voyage to another world. We can see this in the Mesolithic period, where, at a cemetery on the Baltic islands off Denmark, excavations have revealed two people buried within log boats. In Sweden, the cemetery of Skateholm – which we previously visited to see their dog burials – contains a number of burials with soil marks that suggest the outlines of log boat-shaped coffins.

In the Bronze Age, from around 1300 to 700 BCE, 'stone ships' are known from around the Baltic coast. These are human burials surrounded by alignments of stones, forming boat outlines, which were then sealed beneath mounds. Clearly, to these societies the symbolism of the boat shape was extremely important.

In the first millennium of the Common Era, examples of actual boat burials are plentiful. Sutton Hoo is arguably the best-known: the site of two early medieval cemeteries in Suffolk, dating from the sixth to seventh centuries. Within the cemetery are a group of earthen burial mounds, a number of which have been excavated. The most famous is Mound 1. This was excavated in 1939, on the eve of the Second World War, by Basil Brown at the request of the land's owner, Edith Pretty, who afterwards donated the findings to the British Museum where they can still be seen. Although the wood had decayed away, these excavations revealed the presence of iron boat rivets still in situ, and the ghostly imprint of a clinker-built, 27-metre-long boat. This ghost boat had been dragged uphill from the River Deben in the early seventh century, and hauled into a trench. A burial chamber was constructed within the boat, and afterwards it was covered with a mound, two to three metres high.

The wealth of goods discovered in this ship burial is well known, and indicates that it almost certainly provided the resting place of an unknown king. Among the riches was a long and broad sword with an exquisite gold and garnet pommel, and a huge lime-wood shield covered in animal hide and decorated with metal images of wild and fantastical beasts. There was a feather cushion, rare fabrics and furs; fine feasting vessels, and gold with filigree finish. There were coins, as yellow as the sun, from across the Channel, and golden dress accessories set with red Sri Lankan garnets. There were silver bowls from the Byzantine empire, and silver spoons inscribed in Greek. Handsome things that speak of master jewellers and skilful smiths, and of vast movements across land and sea. There were drinking horns and spears, buckets and cauldrons, and a six-stringed lyre in a beaver-skin bag. And carefully wrapped in cloth there was the breathtakingly beautiful Sutton Hoo helmet, with its iconic face mask and eyeless sockets that still stare out on our unfathomable world. These objects drew on, and alluded to, heroic poetry of the day, such as the epic *Beowulf*. Similar burial sites have been found on the continental side of the North Sea, such as those at Gokstad and Oseberg in Norway, although these are of a slightly later date.

The centuries when these boats were buried were formative ones that saw the collapse of the Roman empire in the west and the rise of the Byzantine empire in the east. It was a time of major political events and social changes that ultimately led to the precursors of several modern states and the shaping of the Europe we know today. These boats speak of a connectedness between people and cultures that straddled a great sea.

*

From the earliest prehistory, the sea has played a part in human mobility. Archaeological evidence in the form of distinctive stone tools from Mediterranean islands such as Sicily, Sardinia and Cyprus indicates without any doubt the presence, and therefore the sea-going ability, of early *Homo sapiens*. The discovery of Middle Palaeolithic tools on Crete, dating to between 130,000 and 100,000 years ago, suggests that Neanderthals, stunningly, were probably island-hopping long before modern humans. And incredible open-water crossings were taking place elsewhere in the world: people travelled by boat to Australia from around 50,000 years ago, and very likely earlier.[6]

I find these early sea crossings endlessly fascinating, as they starkly show the skill and cognitive abilities of our early ancestors. Not just in the making of the boats, or even in their navigation and seafaring, as impressive as these are, but in how they show the unmistakably human trait of insatiable, unquenchable wanderlust.

What kind of boats did they travel in? Probably something made of hide or skin stretched over a wicker frame, and propelled with paddles, like the hide-covered coracles that we know were used on lakes in Ireland much later. But this is speculation, because actual evidence of these early prehistoric boats has eluded us. As for paddles: the earliest evidence dates from much later, in the Mesolithic period. A preserved wooden object dating to around 9000 BCE and excavated from Star Carr in Yorkshire might be a paddle. Others have been found elsewhere in Europe.

By the Mesolithic period, seafaring communities that exploited maritime resources were well established. Hide boats no doubt continued to be used, but from this time onwards we find log boats in the archaeological record around Europe and the Mediterranean. These were constructed from hollowed-out tree trunks, in much the same way as the ones found at the much later site of Must Farm in the East Anglian Fens (although the Must Farm boats are more complex in design). Although simple in themselves, log boats could be lashed together to create larger vessels capable of travelling the open seas.

Both hide boats and log boats continued to be used into later prehistory and beyond, carrying people and goods such as the polished jade axe-heads from Alpine regions that arrived in Britain in the Early Neolithic period. The earliest domestic cattle must, likewise, have been brought to the British Isles on boats like this. The original Cowes ferry!

The introduction of bronze tools enabled more sophisticated boat technology such as plank-built vessels, powered by teams of paddlers, of the kind pictured in Nordic Bronze Age rock engravings. Bronze axe, adze and woodworking technology allowed the carving and shaping of oak planks with bevelled edges, creating a close and near water-tight fit. These were not nailed but stitched together using withies of yew. The hull was then made even more water-tight using moss to caulk any gaps. Sewn-plank boats like this from the North Sea region are exclusively Bronze Age in date, developing from around 2000 BCE.

The technique of 'sewing' planks was a strange but important innovation, and probably evolved from, or was an extension of, the stitching of hide boats.[7]

In Britain, we have fairly good archaeological evidence for Bronze Age sewn-plank boats, with part of a plank known from Kilnsea in Yorkshire and fragments from the

Humber at North Ferriby. At this latter site archaeologists found off-cuts of wood, as well as what seem to be shipwrights' tools, suggesting that it may have been part of a prehistoric shipyard. Fragments have also turned up on the Welsh side of the Severn estuary, not far from the Mesolithic footprints we saw at the beginning of the book.

Bronze Age sewn-plank boats created a new mobility that allowed for greater connectivity and the flow of goods. During this time, bronze – and its constituent elements copper and tin – was traded and exchanged across the North Sea, as well as prestige goods, such as gold, jet necklaces, faience jewellery, and objects made of amber, such as beads, spacer plates for necklaces and drinking cups. It is probably not a coincidence that we find evidence developing at the same point in time of both trading in exotic objects and complex, seafaring boats.

Sewn-plank boats would have required a crew of around twenty people, paddling and bailing, as well as a shipwright, an experienced navigator and presumably an aspiring, charismatic leader. The special character, motivation and skills of a leader are taken for granted when we speak about great adventures in the present, or in written history, but it's easy to overlook the need for special individuals to serve as leaders in prehistory too.

*

Our journey together is coming to an end, and there is still one more boat I want to mention before our paths diverge. But first let's look back at the tracks we've made. We started with footprints following footprints, both human and animal. These became trails, which turned into a torrent of trods and roads, leading us on giant human journeys across continents and oceans. Along the way, we have seen that mobility is complex, rich and imbued with meaning and power. It is thoroughly engrained with social activities and cultural practices. And we have seen that movement has been continuous throughout human existence, in the ebb and flow of populations, wave after wave of wanderers washing over the land. We continue these paths with all their intricate, terrifying, interconnected and beautiful movements, because movement is life, and the past was never still.

*

Of nearly twenty sewn-plank boats found in Britain so far, the best preserved is the Dover Bronze Age boat, which is almost complete, and was designed for crossing the Channel. This was found six metres below the streets of Dover in south-east England in 1992, during the construction of a pedestrian underpass. Works that, as coincidence would have it, were associated with a different kind of sea crossing: the Channel Tunnel. The boat dates to the Middle Bronze Age, between 1575 and 1520 BCE, making it Europe's oldest purpose-built sea-going vessel. It is beautiful in every respect, with curved timber planks and twisted yew withies used to stitch the planks together. Astonishingly, the seams are still wedged with Bronze Age moss, beeswax and animal fat for waterproofing.

Constructed out of at least four massive oak trunks, the boat would originally have been up to fifteen metres long. It could have reached speeds of perhaps four knots, and was capable of carrying cargoes of a few tonnes. A small piece of shale inside the boat originally came from

Kimmeridge Bay in Dorset, some 260 km away. It hints, perhaps, at part of a cargo from a former trip. Also found inside the boat was a thin, but surprisingly important, layer of sand. A layer that still makes my hair stand on end when I think of it. Microscopic investigations of this layer demonstrate that it contains grains of glauconite, which are not to be found in the Dover area. Also in the layer are minute marine shell fragments, and much quartz sand. This deposit is beach sand, and it cannot have come from Dover. It was likely carried on board by the prehistoric sailors' feet as they leapt in off some foreign shore – perhaps before taking the boat on its last journey.[8]

We don't know where the sand comes from, or what kind of journey that might have been. Was it close to home, or far afield? Mundane and forgettable, or the adventure of a lifetime? Each discovery we make provides some answers, only to raise a whole new set of questions.

After the boat had been fully excavated and analysed, and after years of conservation work to preserve the timbers for posterity, it was eventually put on display in Dover Museum, where it still is now, behind glass and in its own purpose-built gallery. I've visited the boat several times, my own personal pilgrimage whenever I'm in that part of the country, but I still remember the first, and the profound impact it had. For me, the works of Michelangelo and the divine beauty of the world's finest cathedrals pale by comparison. In my eyes, this boat is worth a thousand of them, because it has the power to transport me instantaneously. To blast me back into deep time, and fly me forwards across land and sea. To look on it is to widen my world and make me more. But then, that is archaeology's superpower!

ACKNOWLEDGEMENTS

Ten years ago, I wrote the introductory chapter to a volume I was editing entitled *Past Mobilities: Archaeological Approaches to Movement and Mobility*, which was published by Ashgate in 2014 (now Routledge). As I wrote that chapter, I knew that what I really wanted to do was to give the subject the time and space it deserved to extend it into a book, and to open the discussion up to wider audiences. In 2016 I was given another chance to think more on mobility when I edited another volume, this time with Thomas Kador, which focused solely on the Neolithic period and was published by Oxbow Books. A third time arose when I contributed a chapter for the festschrift for my friend and former colleague Professor Martin Bell, published by BAR. This book, the one you now hold in your hands, owes much to those chapters, and many of the thoughts, and some of the words, have made their way into this one. I thank Ashgate Publishing, Oxbow Books and BAR.

I carried that desire to write a full-length book about the archaeology of movement with me for a number of years until eventually I stopped walking, sat down, and put pen to paper. I wrote it, on and off, over a number of years. I wholeheartedly thank my current employers, the University of York – especially the wonderful

Professor Nicky Milner – for allowing me the time to complete it.

Footmarks has been in the making for over a decade, and many people have inspired, influenced and helped me in this work, and I have benefited from many lively discussions. Notably these include the attendees at the Theoretical Archaeology Group conference in 2011 (from which the *Past Mobilities* volume arose) and from the Neolithic Studies Group conference in 2012 (from which the *Moving on in Neolithic Studies* volume arose). I have also benefited from numerous ambulatory conversations with many others. There are too many to name all, but some deserve mention, notably those that went the extra mile and read and commented on sections or early drafts of this text. I owe you all a pint or two. These include Ellie Leary (my first reader, always), Ian Armit, Martin Bell, Brian Edwards, Dave Field, Jon Finch, Mel Giles, Elaine Jamieson, Trudi Morgan, Josh Pollard, Rick Schulting and Chris Sayer. Chris died before the book was published, for which I am profoundly sad. I am also grateful for moving conversations with James Snead, Ben Gearey, Matt Edgeworth and Oscar Aldred.

I thank the splendid writer James Canton for reading and commenting on an early draft. I am grateful for walks and chats with two other writers I admire greatly: Julia Blackburn and Amy-Jane Beer. Thank you! I am extremely thankful to The Literary Consultancy, and in particular John Harrison for his wise words and sensible suggestions on a very early draft, before I really knew what I was doing. I sought and gratefully received advice from Anne Furniss, Mary-Ann Ochota and Brian Fagan.

Acknowledgements

I am truly thankful to Michelle Hughes for producing the fine lino-cut illustrations that complement the book so well, and for reading the manuscript and throwing herself into the project. I must also thank the University of York for funding these illustrations (using the YIAF fund), and Kate Giles for drawing my attention to this.

A million thank yous to Jaime Marshall (J.P. Marshall Literary Agency) for taking a punt on this archaeologist, and for friendship, humour and much kindness. And the same to John-Paul Flintoff, editor supremo, for strengthening the book in manifold ways, and for inspiring and pushing me on. And thank you to Icon for publishing this, especially Duncan Heath – I can't imagine a better home for it.

My greatest gratitude, of course, goes to my family – Ellie, Dora and Aggie, and Bard the dog – for allowing me to walk alongside them. Now let's put our boots on once more and get going!

BIBLIOGRAPHY

Adey, P. 2010. *Mobility*. Abingdon: Routledge.

Aldred, O. 2021. *The archaeology of movement*. Abingdon: Routledge.

Allen, V. & Evans, R. 2016. 'Introduction: Roads and writing'. In V. Allen and R. Evans (eds.) *Roadworks. Medieval Britain, medieval roads*, 1–32, Manchester: Manchester University Press (Manchester Medieval Literature and Culture).

Amato, J.A. 2004. *On foot. A history of walking*. New York: New York University Press.

Anthony, D. 2007. *The horse, the wheel, and language. How Bronze Age riders from the Eurasian Steppes shaped the modern world*. Princeton: Princeton University Press.

Appadurai, A. (ed.) 1986. *The Social Life of Things: Commodities in Cultural Perspective*. Cambridge: Cambridge University Press.

Armit, I. & Reich, D. 2021. 'The return of the Beaker folk? Rethinking migration and population change in British prehistory.' *Antiquity* 95(384), 1464–77.

Bailey, D., Whittle, A. & Cummings, V. (ed.) 2005. *(Un)settling the Neolithic*. Oxford: Oxbow Books.

Barnard, H. & Wendrich, W. 2008. *The Archaeology of Mobility. Old World and New World Nomadism*. Los

Angeles, CA: UCLA Cotsen Institute of Archaeology (Cotsen Advanced Seminars 4).

Beaumont, M. 2015. *Nightwalking. A nocturnal history of London. Chaucer to Dickens*. London: Verso.

Bell, M. 2020. *Making one's way in the world. Tracking the movements of prehistoric people*. Oxford: Oxbow Books.

Bell, M. 2007. *Prehistoric Coastal Communities: The Mesolithic in Western Britain*. York: Council for British Archaeology (CBA Research Report 149).

Bell, M., & Leary, J. (2020). 'Pathways to past ways: A positive approach to routeways and mobility.' *Antiquity* 94(377), 1349–59.

Bell, M., Black, S., Maslin, S. & Toms, P. 2020. 'Multi-method solutions of the problem of dating early trackways and associated colluvial sequences.' *Journal of Archaeological Science Reports* 32.

Bellwood, P. 2013. *Ancient migration in global perspective*. Chichester: Wiley-Blackwell.

Bentley, R.A. 2013. 'Mobility and the diversity of Early Neolithic lives: Isotopic evidence from skeletons.' *Journal of Anthropological Archaeology* 32: 303–12.

Beresford, M.W. & Hurst J.G. 1972. *Deserted medieval villages*. London: Lutterworth Press.

Bergerbrant, S., 2019. 'Revisiting the "Egtved girl".' In R. Berge and M. Henriksen, (ed.) *Arkeologi og kulturhistorie fra norskekysten til Østersjøen. Festskrift til professor Birgitta Berglund*. VitArk, Vol. 11. Trondheim: Museumsforlaget, 18–39.

Bickle, P. 2020. 'Thinking Gender Differently: New Approaches to Identity Difference in the Central

European Neolithic.' *Cambridge Archaeological Journal* 30(2), 201–18.

Bil, A. 1990. *The Shieling, 1600–1840: The case of the Central Scottish Highlands*. Edinburgh: John Donald Publishers Ltd.

Bird, M.I., O'Grady, D. & Ulm, S. 2016. 'Humans, water, and the colonization of Australia.' *PNAS* 113(41), 11477–82.

Bishop, M.C. 2014. *The Secret History of the Roman Roads of Britain*. Barnsley: Pen & Sword Military.

Boivin, N. & Owac, M.A. (ed.) 2004. *Soils, stones and symbols. Cultural perceptions of the mineral world*. London: UCL Press.

Bonnett, A. 2015. 'Walking through memory: Critical nostalgia and the city.' In T. Richardson (ed.) *Walking inside out. Contemporary British psychogeography*, 75–87. London: Rowman & Littlefield International Ltd.

Boulgouris, N.V., Hatzinakos, D. & Plataniotis, K.N. 2005. 'Gait recognition: A challenging signal processing technology for biometric identification.' *IEEE Signal Processing Magazine*, November 2005, 78–90.

Bowden, M. & Herring, P. (ed.) 2021. *Transhumance. Papers from the International Association of Landscape Archaeology Conference, Newcastle upon Tyne, 2018*. Oxford: Archaeopress.

Bozell, J.R. 1988. 'Changes in the role of the dog in protohistoric-historic Pawnee culture.' *Plains Anthropologist* 33(119), 95–111.

Brace, S., Diekmann, Y. & Booth, T.J. *et al.* 2019. 'Ancient genomes indicate population replacement in Early Neolithic Britain.' *Nature Ecology & Evolution* 3, 765–71.

Bradley, R. 1999. 'Pilgrimage in prehistoric Britain?' In J. Stopford (ed.) *Pilgrimage explored.* York: York Medieval Press.

Bradley, R., Jones, A., Nordenborg Myhre, L. & Sackett, H. 2002. 'Sailing through stone: carved ships and the rock face at Revheim, Southwest Norway.' *Norwegian Archaeological Review* 35(2), 109–18.

Bradley, R., Meredith, P., Smith, J. & Edmonds, M. 1992. 'Rock physics and the Neolithic axe trade in Great Britain.' *Archaeometry* 34(2), 223–33.

Brennand, M., Taylor, M., Ashwin, T., *et al.* 2003. 'The Survey and Excavation of a Bronze Age Timber Circle at Holme-next-the-Sea, Norfolk, 1998–9.' *Proceedings of the Prehistoric Society* 69, 1–84.

Brigham, A. 2015. *American road narratives. Reimagining mobility in literature and film.* Charlottesville: University of Virginia Press.

Brittain, M. and Overton, N. 2013. 'The Significance of Others: A Prehistory of Rhythm and Interspecies Participation.' *Society & Animals* 21, 134–49.

Brody, H. 2001. *The Other Side of Eden. Hunters, farmers, and the shaping of the world.* London, Faber & Faber.

Brophy, K. 2015. *Reading Between the Lines. The Neolithic Cursus Monuments of Scotland.* London: Routledge.

Brown, K.A. 2014. 'Women on the Move. The DNA evidence for female mobility and exogamy in prehistory.' In J. Leary (ed.) *Past Mobilities. Archaeological Approaches to Movement and Mobility,* 155–73. Farnham: Ashgate.

Brumm, A. 2004. 'An axe to grind. Symbolic considerations of stone axe use in ancient Australia.' In N. Boivin &

M.A. Owac (eds.) *Soils, stones and symbols. Cultural perceptions of the mineral world*, 143–63. London: UCL Press.

Chadwick, A. 2016a. 'Foot-fall and Hoof-hit. Agencies, Movements, Materialities, and Identities; and Later Prehistoric and Romano-British Trackways.' *Cambridge Archaeological Journal* 26(1), 93–120.

Chadwick, A. 2016b. 'The Stubborn Light of Things. Landscape, Relational Agency, and Linear Earthworks in Later Prehistoric Britain.' *European Journal of Archaeology* 19(2), 245–78.

Chadwick, A. 2013. 'Some fishy things about scales: Macro- and microapproaches to later prehistoric and Romano-British field systems.' *Landscapes* 14(1), 13–32.

Chadwick, A. 2007. 'Trackways, hooves and memory-days – human and animal movements and memories around the Iron Age and Romano-British rural landscapes of the English north midlands.' In V. Cummings & Johnston, R. (eds.) *Prehistoric journeys*, 131–52. Oxford: Oxbow Books.

Chatwin, B. 1987 [1998]. *The Songlines*. London: Vintage Books.

Chatwin, B. 1988 [2005]. *What Am I Doing Here*. London: Vintage Books.

Clark, P. (ed.) 2004. *The Dover Bronze Age boat*. Swindon: English Heritage.

Coble, T., Selin, S.W. & Erickson, B.B. 2003. 'Hiking alone: Understanding fear, negotiation strategies and leisure experience.' *Journal of Leisure Research* 35(1), 1–22.

Cohen, J.H. & Sirkeci, I. 2011. *Cultures of migration. The global nature of contemporary mobility*. Austin: University of Texas Press.

Coles, B. & Coles, J. 1986. *Sweet track to Glastonbury*. London: Thames and Hudson.

Cook, M. 1998. *Medieval bridges*. Princes Risborough: Shire Publications Ltd.

Costello, E. 2020. *Transhumance and the making of Ireland's uplands. 1550–1900*. Woodbridge: The Boydell Press.

Costello, E. 2018. 'Temporary freedoms? Ethnoarchaeology of female herders at seasonal sites in northern Europe.' *World Archaeology* 50(1), 165–84.

Cunliffe, B. 2017. *On the ocean. The Mediterranean and the Atlantic from prehistory to AD 1500*. Oxford: Oxford University Press.

Cresswell, T. 2006. *On the move. Mobility in the modern western world*. Abingdon: Routledge.

Cribb, R. 1991. *Nomads in archaeology*. Cambridge: Cambridge University Press.

Darling, J.A. 2009. 'O'odham trails and the archaeology of space.' In Snead, J.E., Erickson, C.L. & Darling, J.A. (eds.) *Landscapes of movement. Trails, paths, and roads in anthropological perspective*, 61–83. Philadelphia: University of Pennsylvania Press.

Davies, T.G., Pomeroy, E., Shaw, C.N. & Stock, J.T. 2014. 'Mobility and the Skeleton: A Biomechanical View.' In Leary, J. (ed.) *Past Mobilities: Archaeological Approaches to Movement and Mobility*, 129–53. Farnham: Ashgate.

Davies, P., Robb, J.G. & Ladbrook, D. 2003. 'Woodland clearance in the Mesolithic: The social aspects.' *Antiquity* 79, 280–88.

Deakin, R. 2008. *Notes from Walnut Tree Farm*. London: Hamish Hamilton.

Debord, G. 1956 [1981]. *Theory of the Dérive*. Trans. Ken Knabb. Situationist International Anthology. Berkeley: Bureau of Public Secrets.

DeSilva, J. 2021. *First steps. How walking upright made us human*. London: William Collins.

De Waal, F. 2016. *Are we smart enough to know how smart animals are?* London: Granta.

Dickson, J.H., Oeggl, K. & Handley, L.L. 2003. 'The Iceman Reconsidered.' *Scientific American* 288(5), 70–79.

Dittmar, J.M., Mitchell, P.D., Cessford, C., Inskip, J.E. Robb, S.A. 2021. 'Fancy shoes and painful feet: Hallux valgus and fracture risk in medieval Cambridge, England.' *International Journal of Paleopathology* 35, 90–100.

Ó'Dubhthaigh N. 1983. 'Summer pasture in Donegal.' *Folk Life. Journal of Ethnological Studies* 22(1), 42–54.

Dunn, S. 2020. 'Folklore in the landscape: The case of the corpse paths.' *Time and Mind* 13(3), 245–65.

Eckardt, H. 2010. 'A long way from home: Diaspora communities in Roman Britain.' In H. Eckardt (ed.) *Roman diasporas: Archaeological approaches to mobility and diversity in the Roman Empire*, 99–130. Portsmouth, RI: Journal of Roman Archaeology (Supplementary Series 78).

Eckardt, H., Müldner, G., & Lewis, M. 2014. 'People on the move in Roman Britain.' *World Archaeology* 46(4), 534–50.

Edensor, T. 2000. 'Walking in the British countryside: Reflexivity, embodied practices and ways to escape.' *Body & Society* 6(3–4), 81–106.

Edgeworth, M. 2014. 'Enmeshments of shifting landscapes and embodied movements of people and animals.' In Leary J. (ed.) *Past Mobilities: Archaeological Approaches to Movement and Mobility*, 49–61. Farnham: Ashgate.

Edgeworth, M. 2011. *Fluid pasts. Archaeology of flow*. London: Bloomsbury Academic (Debates in Archaeology).

Elborough, T. 2016. *A walk in the park. The life and times of a people's institution*. London: Jonathan Cape.

Evans, C.P. 2008. *Trods of the North York Moors. A gazetteer of flagged paths*. Scarborough: Scarborough Archaeological and Historical Society (Research Report 13).

Evans, C. and Knight, M. 2000. 'A fenland delta: later prehistoric land use in the lower Ouse reaches.' M. Dawson (ed.) *Prehistoric, Roman and post-Roman landscapes in the Great Ouse Valley*, 87–106. York: Council for British Archaeology (Research Report 119).

Evans, J. 2003. *Environmental archaeology and the social order*. London: Routledge.

Everitt, A. 2000. 'Common Land.' In J. Thirsk (ed.) *The English Rural Landscape*. Oxford: Oxford University Press.

Everson, P. 2003. 'Medieval gardens and designed landscapes.' In R. Wilson-North (ed.) *The lie of the land*.

Aspects of the archaeology and history of the designed landscape in the south west of England, 24–33. Exeter: The Mint Press.

Fairclough, G. 1992. 'Meaningful constructions – spatial and functional analysis of medieval buildings.' *Antiquity* 66, 348–66.

Farnell, B. 1994. 'Ethno-graphics and the moving body.' *MAN* (N.S.) 29(4), 929–74.

Farnell, B. 1996. 'Metaphors we move by.' *Visual Anthropology* 8(2–4), 311–35.

Farnell, B. 1999. 'Moving body, acting selves.' *Annual Review of Anthropology*, Vol. 28, 341–73.

Farnell, B. and Wood, R.N. 2011. 'Performing precision and the limits of observation.' In T. Ingold (ed.) *Redrawing Anthropology. Materials, Movements, Lines*, 91—113. Farnham: Ashgate.

Faulkner, P.A. 1963. 'Castle planning in the fourteenth century.' *Archaeological Journal* 120(1), 215–35.

Ferentinos, G., Gkioni, M., Geraga, M., & Papatheodorou G. 2012. 'Early seafaring activity in the southern Ionian Islands, Mediterranean Sea.' *Journal of Archaeological Science* 39, 2167–76.

Field, D. 1989. 'Tranchet axes and Thames picks: Mesolithic core-tools from the West London Thames.' *Transactions of the London and Middlesex Archaeological Society* 40, 1–46.

Fitzpatrick, A.P. 2011. *The Amesbury Archer and the Boscombe Bowmen. Bell Beaker Burials on Boscombe Down, Amesbury, Wiltshire*. Salisbury: Wessex Archaeology.

Fleming, A. 2009. 'The making of a medieval road: The Monk's Trod routeway, mid Wales.' *Landscapes* 1, 77–100.

Fleming, A. 1988. *The Dartmoor Reaves. Investigating prehistoric land divisions*. London: B.T. Batsford.

Foubert, L., & Breeze, D.J. 2014. 'Mobility in the Roman Empire.' In J. Leary (ed.) *Past Mobilities. Archaeological Approaches to Movement and Mobility*, 175–86. Farnham: Ashgate.

Fowler, C. 2004. *The archaeology of personhood. An anthropological approach*. London: Routledge (Themes in Archaeology).

Fowler, P. 2000. *Landscape plotted and pieced: Landscape history and local archaeology in Fyfield and Overton, Wiltshire*. London: Society of Antiquaries of London.

Fox, H. 2012. *Dartmoor's alluring uplands. Transhumance and pastoral management in the Middle Ages*. Exeter: University of Exeter Press.

Frei, K.M., Villa, C., Jørkov, M.L. *et al.* 2017. 'A matter of months: High precision migration chronology of a Bronze Age female.' *PLoS ONE* 12(6).

Fulford, M. and Timby, J. 2000. *Late Iron Age and Roman Silchester: Excavation on the site of the Forum/Basilica, 1977, 1980–86*. London: Britannia Monograph Series 15.

Fumerton, P. 2006. *Unsettled. The Culture of Mobility and the Working Poor in Early Modern England*. Chicago: University of Chicago Press.

Gagnol, L. 2021. 'Identify, search and monitor by tracks: Elements of analysis of pastoral know-how in Saharan-

Sahelian societies.' In A. Pastoors & T. Lenssen-Erz (eds.) *Reading prehistoric human tracks. Methods & material.* Switzerland: Springer, 363–83.

Georgiou, L., Dunmore, C.J., Bardo, A., Buck, L.T., Hublin, J-J., Pahr, D.H., Stratford, D., Synek, A., Kivell, T.L. & Skinner, M.M. 2020. 'Evidence for habitual climbing in a Pleistocene hominin in South Africa.' *Proceedings of the National Academy of Sciences* 117, 8416–23.

Gilchrist, R. 2012. *Medieval life: Archaeology and the life course.* Woodbridge: Boydell & Brewer.

Gilchrist, R. 2013. 'The materiality of medieval heirlooms: From biographical to sacred objects.' In H.P. Hahn and H. Weiss (eds.) *Mobility, Meaning and Transformations of Things. Shifting contexts of material culture through time and space*, 170–82. Oxford: Oxbow Books.

Gilchrist, R. 1999. *Gender and archaeology: Contesting the past.* London: Routledge.

Gilchrist, R. and Sloane, B. 2005. *Requiem: The Medieval Monastic Cemetery in Britain.* London: Museum of London Archaeology Service.

Giles, M. 2020. *Bog bodies. Face to face with the past.* Manchester: Manchester University Press.

Giles, M. 2012. *A forged glamour. Landscape, identity and material culture in the Iron Age.* Oxford: Windgather Press.

Goffman, E. 1959. *The presentation of self in everyday life.* London: Penguin Books.

González-Ruibal, A. 2013. 'Houses of resistance: Time and materiality among the Mao of Ethiopia.' In H.P. Hahn and H. Weiss (eds.) *Mobility, Meaning and Transformations of Things. Shifting contexts of material culture through time and space*, 15–36. Oxford: Oxbow Books.

Gooch, P. 2008. 'Feet following hooves.' In T. Ingold and J. L. Vergunst (eds.) *Ways of walking: Ethnography and practice on foot*, 67–80. Farnham: Ashgate (Anthropological Studies of Creativity and Perception).

Gooder, J. 2007. 'Excavation of a Mesolithic house at East Barns, East Lothian, Scotland: An interim view.' In C. Waddington and K. Pedersen (eds.) *Mesolithic studies in the North Sea basin and beyond. Proceedings of a conference held at Newcastle in 2003*, 49–59. Oxford: Oxbow Books.

Green, C. 2004. 'Evidence of a marine environment associated with the Dover boat.' In P. Clark (ed.) *The Dover Bronze Age Boat in context. Society and water transport in prehistoric Europe*. Oxford: Oxbow Books.

Gros, F. 2014. *A philosophy of walking*. Trans. John Howe. London: Verso.

Hahn, H.P. and Weiss, H. (ed.) 2013. *Mobility, meaning and transformations of things. Shifting contexts of material culture through time and space*. Oxford: Oxbow Books.

Harding, J. 2003. *Henge monuments of the British Isles*. Stroud: Tempus.

Harris, A. 2015. *Weatherland. Writers and artists under English skies*. London: Thames & Hudson.

Harrison, M. 2016a. *Rain. Four walks in English weather*. London: Faber & Faber.

Harrison, M. (ed.) 2016b. *Seasons. An anthology of changing seasons*. London: Elliott & Thompson.

Harrison, S. 2003. 'The Icknield Way: Some queries.' *Archaeological Journal* 160, 1–22.

Hellström, M. 2015. 'Fast movement through the city: Ideals, stereotypes and city planning.' In I. Östenberg, S. Malmberg, & J. Bjørnebye, *The moving city. Processions, passages and promenades in Ancient Rome*, 47–57. London: Bloomsbury Academic.

Helms, M.W. 1988. *Ulysses' sail. An ethnographic odyssey of power, knowledge, and geographical distance*. Princeton: Princeton University Press.

Hindle, P. 2016. 'Sources for the English medieval road system.' In V. Allen and R. Evans (eds.) *Roadworks. Medieval Britain, medieval roads*, 33–49. Manchester: Manchester University Press (Manchester Medieval Literature and Culture).

Hindle, P. 1998. *Medieval roads and tracks*. Oxford: Shire Publications Ltd.

Honeychurch, W. and Makarewicz, C.A. 2016. 'The archaeology of pastoral nomadism.' *Annual Review of Anthropology* 45, 341–59.

Hosfield, R. 2020. *The earliest Europeans – a year in the life: seasonal survival strategies in the Lower Palaeolithic*. Oxford: Oxbow Books.

Houseman, M. 1998. 'Painful places: Ritual encounters with one's homelands.' *The Journal of the Royal Anthropological Institute* 4(3), 447–67.

Hulme, M. 2017. *Weathered. Cultures of climate change*. London: SAGE.

Ingold, T. 2011. *Being alive. Essays on movement, knowledge and description*. Abingdon: Routledge.

Ingold, T. 2009. 'Against space: Place, movement, knowledge.' In *Boundless Worlds. An Anthropological Approach to Movement*, P.W. Kirby (ed.). Oxford: Berghahn, 29–43.

Ingold, T. 2004. 'Culture on the ground. The world perceived through feet.' *Journal of Material Culture*, 9(3), 315–40.

Ingold, T. 2000. *The perception of the environment. Essays in livelihood, dwelling and skill*. London: Routledge.

Ingold, T. & Vergunst, J.L. 2008. 'Introduction.' In T. Ingold & J. L. Vergunst (eds.) *Ways of walking. Ethnography and practice on foot*, 1–19. Fareham: Ashgate (Anthropological Studies of Creativity and Perception).

James, W. (2003) *The Ceremonial animal. A new portrait of anthropology*. Oxford, Oxford University Press.

Jamieson, E. & Lane, R. 2015 'Monuments, Mobility and Medieval Perceptions of Designed Landscapes: The Pleasance, Kenilworth.' *Medieval Archaeology* 59(1), 255–71.

Jarman, C. 2021. *River Kings. A new history of the Vikings from Scandinavia to the Silk Roads*. London: William Collins.

Johnson, M. 2002. *Behind the castle gate. From medieval to Renaissance*. London: Routledge.

Johnson, M. 1996. *An archaeology of capitalism*. Oxford: Blackwell.

Kashner, S. 2013. 'Fever Pitch.' *Vanity Fair*, 15 August 2013.

Kelly, R. 1992. 'Mobility/sedentism: Concepts, archaeological measures and effects.' *Annual Review of Anthropology* 21, 43–66.

Kelly, R. 1995. *The foraging spectrum*. London, Smithsonian Institution Press.

Kern, H. 2000. *Through the labyrinth: Designs and meanings over 5,000 years*. Trans. Abigail Clay. Munich: Prestel.

Klein, J. 1920. 'The Mesta: A study in Spanish economic history, 1273–1836.' Harvard, MA: Harvard University Press.

Knight, M., Ballantyne, R., Robinson Zeki, I., & Gibson, D. 2019. 'The Must Farm pile-dwelling settlement.' *Antiquity* 93(369), 645–63.

Kohn, E. 2013. *How forests think. Toward an anthropology beyond the human*. Berkeley: University of California Press.

Krause, J. & Trappe, T. 2021. *A short history of humanity. How migration made us who we are*. London: W.H. Allen.

Labarge, M.W. 1982. *Medieval travellers: The rich and restless*. London: Hamish Hamilton.

Lakoff, G. & Johnson, M. 1980. *Metaphors we live by*. Chicago: University of Chicago Press.

Lane Fox, R. 2008. *Travelling heroes: Greeks and their myths in the epic age of Homer*. London: Allen Lane.

Langlands, A. 2019. *The ancient ways of Wessex. Travel and communication in an early medieval landscape*. Oxford: Windgather Press.

Larsson, L. 1990. 'Dogs in Fraction – Symbols in Action.' In P. Vermeersch and P. van Peer (eds.), *Contributions to the Mesolithic in Europe*, 161–7. Leuven: Leuven University Press.

Leary, J. 2015. *The Remembered Land. Surviving sea-level rise after the last Ice Age*. London: Bloomsbury (Debates in Archaeology series).

Leary, J. (ed.) 2014. *Past Mobilities: Archaeological Approaches to Movement and Mobility*. Farnham: Ashgate.

Leary, J. 2010. 'Silbury Hill: a monument in motion.' In Leary, J., Darvill, T., Field, D. (ed.) 2010. *Round Mounds and Monumentality in the British Neolithic and Beyond*. Oxford: Oxbow Books/Neolithic Studies Group Seminar Papers 10, 139–52.

Leary, J. and Field, D. (2012). 'Journeys and juxtapositions. Marden henge and the view from the Vale.' In Gibson, A. (ed.) *Enclosing the Neolithic. Recent studies in Britain and Europe*, 55–65. Oxford: BAR (International Series 2440).

Leary, J. and Field, D. 2010. *The story of Silbury Hill*. Swindon: English Heritage publishing.

Leary, J. and Kador, T. (ed.) 2016. *Moving on in Neolithic studies: Understanding mobile lives*. Oxford: Oxbow Publishing (Neolithic Studies Group Seminar Papers).

Lee, J. and Ingold, T. 2006. 'Fieldwork on foot: Perceiving, routing, socializing.' In S. Coleman and P. Collins (eds.) *Locating the Field. Space, Place and Context in Anthropology*, 67–85. Oxford: Berg.

Librado, P., Khan, N., Fages, A. *et al.* 2021. 'The origins and spread of domestic horses from the Western Eurasian steppes.' *Nature* 598, 634–40.

Liebenberg, L. 1990. *The art of tracking. The origin of science*. Cape Town: Creda Press.

Lewis, N. 2000. 'The climbing body, nature and the experience of modernity.' *Body & Society* 6(3–4), 58–80.

Loveday, R. 2016. 'Monuments to mobility? Investigating cursus patterning in southern Britain.' In J. Leary and T. Kador (eds.) *Moving on in Neolithic studies. Understanding mobile lives*, 67–109. Oxford: Oxbow Books.

Loveday, R. 1998. 'Double entrance henges – routes to the past?' In A. Gibson and D. Simpson (eds.) *Essays in honour of Aubrey Burl: Prehistoric ritual and religion*, 14–31. Stroud: Sutton Publishing.

Mabey, R. 2013. *Turned out Nice Again: Living with weather*. London: Profile Books.

Macfarlane, R. 2012. *The Old Ways: A journey on foot*. London: Penguin Books.

Macfarlane, R., Richards, D., Donwood, S. 2014. *Holloway*. London: Faber & Faber.

Macnaghten, P. and Urry, J. 2000. 'Bodies in the woods.' *Body & Society* 6(3–4), 166–82.

Malchik, A. 2019. *A walking life: Reclaiming our health and our freedom one step at a time*. New York: Da Capo Press.

Malim, T. & Hayes, L. 2011. *The Road. British Archaeology* 120, 14–19.

Manco, P. 2013. *Ancestral journeys. The peopling of Europe from the first venturers to the Vikings.* London: Thames & Hudson.

Maraszek, R. 2009. *The Nebra Sky-disc. Kleine Reihe zu den Himmelswegen,* 2 (Halle, Germany). (English version by B. O'Connor & D. Tucker).

Margetts, A. 2021. *The wandering herd. The medieval cattle economy of south-east England c. 450–1450.* Oxford: Windgather Press.

Mauss, M. 1954. *The gift. Forms and functions of exchange in archaic societies.* 2011 edition. Trans. Ian Cunnison. Illinois: The Free Press.

Mauss, M. 1973 [1935]. 'Techniques of the body.' *Economy and Society* 2(1), 70–88.

Michael, M. 2000. 'These boots are made for walking …: Mundane technology, the body and human-environment relations.' *Body & Society* 6(3–4), 107–26.

Mitchell, P. 2015. *Horse Nations. The worldwide impact of the horse on indigenous societies post-1492.* Oxford: Oxford University Press.

Montgomery, J., Budd, P. & Evans, J. 2000. 'Reconstructing the lifetime movements of ancient people: a Neolithic case study from southern England.' *European Journal of Archaeology* 3, 370–85.

Moran, J. 2009. *On Roads: A hidden history.* London: Profile Books.

Morrison, S.S. 2000. *Women Pilgrims in Medieval England: Private Piety as Public Performance.* London: Routledge (Routledge Research in Medieval Studies 3).

Mortimer, J.R. 1895. 'The grouping of barrows, and its bearing on the religious beliefs of the ancient Britons.' *Transactions of the East Riding Antiquarian Society* 3, 53–62.

Moxham, R. 2001. *The great hedge of India*. London: Constable.

Nicholson, G. 2008. *The Lost Art of Walking: The History, Science, Philosophy, and Literature of Pedestrianism*. New York: Riverhead.

Nielsen, N., Henriksen, P., Mortensen, M., *et al.* 2021. 'The last meal of Tollund Man: New analyses of his gut content.' *Antiquity* 95(383).

Noble, G. 2017. *Woodland in the Neolithic of Northern Europe. The forest as ancestor*. Cambridge: Cambridge University Press.

Norman, K., Inglis, J., Clarkson, C., Faith, J.T., Shulmeister, J., & Harris, D. 2018. 'An early colonisation pathway into northwest Australia 70–60,000 years ago.' *Quaternary Science Reviews* 180, 229–39.

Ohler, N. 1989. *The Medieval Traveller*. (Trans. C. Hillier). Woodbridge: The Boydell Press.

Olalde, I., Brace, S., Allentoft, M. *et al*. 2018. 'The Beaker phenomenon and the genomic transformation of northwest Europe.' *Nature* 555, 190–6.

Olsen, B. 2013. *In defence of things. Archaeology and the ontology of objects*. Maryland: AltaMira Press.

Olsen, B., Shanks, M., Webmoor, T. & Witmoor, C. 2012. *Archaeology. The discipline of things.*

Berkeley and Los Angeles: University of California Press.

Oma, K.A. 2010. 'Between trust and domination: social contracts between humans and animals.' *World Archaeology* 42(2), 175–87.

O'Mara, S. 2019. *In Praise of Walking. The new science of how we walk and why it is good for us*. London: The Bodley Head.

O'Sullivan, T.M. 2011. *Walking in Roman culture*. Cambridge: Cambridge University Press.

Östenberg, I., Malmberg, S. and Bjørnebye, J. 2015. *The moving city. Processions, passages and promenades in Ancient Rome*. London: Bloomsbury Academic.

Östenberg, I. 2015. 'Power walks: Aristocratic escorted movements in Republican Rome.' In I. Östenberg, S. Malmberg, and J. Bjørnebye, *The moving city. Processions, passages and promenades in Ancient Rome*, 13–22. London: Bloomsbury Academic.

Overton, N.J. and Hamilakis, Y. 2013. 'A manifesto for a social zooarchaeology. Swans and other beings in the Mesolithic.' *Archaeological Dialogues* 20(2) 111–36.

Pastoors, A. & Lenssen-Erz, T. (eds.) 2021. *Reading prehistoric human tracks. Methods & material*. Switzerland: Springer.

Patterson, N., Isakov, M., Booth, T. *et al*. 2022. 'Large-scale migration into Britain during the Middle to Late Bronze Age.' *Nature* 601, 588–94.

Pétrequin, P., Cassen, S., Errera, M., Klassen, L., Pétrequin, A.-M., & Sheridan, A. 2013. 'The value of things: the production and circulation of alpine jade axes during the 5th-4th millennia in a European perspective.' In T. Kerig, A. Zimmermann (eds.), *Economic Archaeology: From Structure to Performance in European Archaeology*, 65–82.

Pollard, J. 2017. 'The Uffington White Horse geoglyph as sun-horse.' *Antiquity* 91(356), 406–20.

Pollard, J. 1995. 'Inscribing Space: Formal Deposition at the Later Neolithic Monument of Woodhenge, Wiltshire.' *Proceedings of the Prehistoric Society* 61, 137–56.

Pollard, J. 1992. 'The Sanctuary, Overton Hill, Wiltshire: A re-examination.' *Proceedings of the Prehistoric Society* 58, 213–26.

Prestwich, M. 2016. 'The royal itinerary and roads in England under Edward I.' In V. Allen and R. Evans (eds.) *Roadworks. Medieval Britain, medieval roads*, 177–97, Manchester: Manchester University Press (Manchester Medieval Literature and Culture).

Pryor, F. 2002. *Seahenge: A Quest for Life and Death in Bronze Age Britain*. London: HarperCollins.

Pryor, F. 2001. *The Flag Fen Basin: Archaeology and environment of a Fenland landscape*. London: English Heritage.

Püntenera, A.G. and Moss S. 2010. 'Ötzi, the Iceman and his Leather Clothes.' *Chimia* 64, 315–20.

Pye, M. 2014. *The edge of the world. How the North Sea made us who we are*. London: Penguin Books.

Rackham, O. 1986. *The History of the Countryside*. London: J.M. Dent.

Rackham, O. 1976. *Trees and Woodland in the British Landscape*. London: J.M. Dent.

Reich, D. 2018. *Who we are and how we got here. Ancient DNA and the new science of the human past*. Oxford: Oxford University Press.

Reynolds, A. and Langlands, A. 2011. 'Travel as communication: A consideration of overland journeys in Anglo-Saxon England.' *World Archaeology* 43, 410–27.

Richards, C. 1996a. 'Henges and water: Towards an elemental understanding of monumentality and landscape in Late Neolithic Britain.' *Journal of Material Culture* 1(3), 313–36.

Richards, C. 1996b. 'Monuments as landscape: Creating the centre of the world in Late Neolithic Orkney.' *World Archaeology* 28(2), 190–208.

Richardson, T. (ed.) 2015. *Walking inside out. Contemporary British psychogeography*. London: Rowman & Littlefield International Ltd.

Rudenko, S.I. 1970. *Frozen tombs of Siberia: The Pazyryk burials of Iron Age horsemen*. Berkeley and Los Angeles: University of California Press.

Sauer, M.M. 2016. 'The function of material and spiritual roads in the English eremitic tradition.' In V. Allen and R. Evans (eds.) *Roadworks. Medieval Britain, medieval roads*, 157–76, Manchester: Manchester University Press (Manchester Medieval Literature and Culture).

Saunders, D. 2021. *The cursus enigma. Prehistoric cattle and cursus alignments*. Oxford: Peter Lang.

Schofield, J. 2009. 'Landscape with Snow.' *Landscapes* 10(2), 1–18.

Sennett, R. 2011. *The foreigner. Two essays on exile*. London: Notting Hill Editions.

Shah, S. 2020. *The Next Great Migration. The Story of Movement on a Changing Planet*. London: Bloomsbury.

Sharples, N. 2010. *Social relations in later prehistory. Wessex in the first millennium BC*. Oxford: Oxford University Press.

Sheets-Johnstone, M. 2011. *The primacy of movement. Expanded second edition*. Philadelphia: John Benjamins Publishing Company (Advance in Consciousness Research 82).

Simonsen, M.F. 2019. 'Medieval Pilgrim Badges: Souvenirs or Valuable Charismatic Objects?' In M. Vedeler, I.M. Røstad, E.S. Kristoffersen, Z.T. Glørstad (eds.), *Charismatic Objects: From Roman Times to the Middle Ages*, 169–96. Oslo: Cappelen Damm Akademisk.

Solnit, R. 2005. *A Field Guide to Getting Lost*. London: Penguin Books.

Solnit, R. 2001. *Wanderlust: A History of Walking*. London: Verso.

Strohmayer, U. 2011. 'Bridges: Different conditions of mobile possibilities.' In T. Cresswell and P. Merriman (eds.) *Geographies of Mobilities: Practices, Spaces, Subjects*, 119–35. Farnham: Ashgate.

Thomas, G.M. 2006. 'Women in public: The display of femininity in the parks of Paris'. In A. D'Souza and T. McDonough (eds.) *The invisible flâneuse. Gender, public space, and visual culture in nineteenth-century Paris*, 32–48. Manchester: Manchester University Press.

Thoreau, H.D. 1854 [1995]. *Walden; or, life in the woods*. New York: Dover Publications.

Toulson, S. 2005. *The Drovers*. Oxford: Shire Publications Ltd.

Urry, J. 2007. *Mobilities*. Cambridge: Polity.

Van de Noort, R. 2011. *North Sea Archaeologies. A maritime biography, 10,000 BC–AD 1500*. Oxford: Oxford University Press.

Vikatou, I., Hoogland, M.L.P., & Waters-Rist, A.L. 2017. 'Osteochondritis Dissecans of skeletal elements of the foot in a 19th century rural farming community from The Netherlands.' *International Journal of Paleopathology* Vol. 19, 53–63.

Vyner, B. 2007. 'A Great North Route in Neolithic and Bronze Age Yorkshire: The evidence of landscape and monuments.' *Landscapes* 1, 69–84.

Waddington, C. 2007. 'Rethinking Mesolithic settlement and a case study from Howick.' In C. Waddington and K. Pedersen (eds.) *Mesolithic studies in the North Sea basin and beyond. Proceedings of a conference held at Newcastle in 2003*, 101–13. Oxford: Oxbow Books.

Woodman, P.C. 1985. *Excavations at Mount Sandel 1973–77*. Belfast: Her Majesty's Stationery Office (Northern Ireland Archaeological Monographs 2).

Webb, D. 2000. *Pilgrimage in Medieval England*. London: Hambledon and London.

Whittle, A. 2003. *The archaeology of people. Dimensions of Neolithic life*. London: Routledge.

Whittle, A. 1997. 'Moving on and moving around: Neolithic settlement mobility.' In P. Topping (ed.) *Neolithic landscapes*, 15–22. Oxford: Oxbow Books (Neolithic Studies Group Seminar Paper 2).

Widell, B. 2017. 'The monastic lifeworld: memories and narratives of landscapes of early medieval monasticism in Argyll, Scotland.' *Landscapes* 18, 4–18.

Will, C. 2017. *Lovers and strangers. An immigrant history of post-war Britain*. London: Allen Lane.

Williams, T.J. 2017. *Walking with cattle. In search of the last drovers of Uist*. Edinburgh: Birlinn.

Williamson, T.M. 2000. 'Understanding enclosure.' *Landscape* 1, 56–79.

Winchester, S. 2010. *Atlantic. A vast ocean of a million stories*. London: Harper Press.

Wittering, S. 2013. *Ecology and enclosure. The effect of enclosure on society, farming and the environment in South Cambridgeshire, 1798–1850*. Oxford: Windgather Press.

Yates, D. 2007. *Land, power and prestige: Bronze Age field systems in southern England*. Oxford: Oxbow Books.

Yates, D. 2001. 'Bronze Age agricultural intensification in the Thames valley and estuary.' In J. Brück (ed.) *Bronze Age landscapes: Tradition and transformation*, 65–82. Oxford: Oxbow Books.

Zeaman, J. 2011. *Dog walks man. A six-legged odyssey*. Connecticut: Lyons Press.

NOTES

1 The stillness of the past

1. For Marden, see Leary & Field 2012. For Silbury, see Leary 2010, and Leary & Field 2010.
2. See Aldred 2021; Leary 2014; Bell & Leary 2020 for more on this. See Urry 2007, Adey 2010 and Cresswell 2006 for a wider discussion of this beyond archaeology.
3. This quote is from Ingold 2011, 148.
4. See some of the anthropological literature for more on this: Ingold 2009, 2011; Lee & Ingold 2006; James 2003.

2 Moving matters

1. See Sheets-Johnstone 2011 for a discussion of mobility and many of the themes in this chapter.
2. Lakoff & Johnson 1980. Also see Farnell 1996.
3. See O'Mara 2019 and Malchik 2019 for more on this.
4. See Gros 2014 for an entertaining account of the themes in this and subsequent paragraphs.
5. For 'man's real home ...', see Chatwin 1988, 273. For 'The act of journeying ...', see Chatwin 1988, 221. For the Deakin quote, see Deakin 2008, 240. Also see: Solnit 2001; Macfarlane 2012; Macfarlane *et al.* 2014; Nicholson 2008.

6. See, for example, Davies *et al.* 2014.
7. See, for example, Bentley 2013 and Montgomery *et al.* 2000.

3 Printmaking

1. Bell 2020 provides a good, authoritative summary of archaeological footprint tracks.
2. See DeSilva 2021 for an excellent discussion of this.
3. This and the subsequent examples of footprint tracks can all be found in the wonderful, open access, edited volume, Pastoors & Lenssen-Erz 2021. Also see Bell 2020 for a good summary of footprints, and Bell 2007 for more on the Severn Estuary footprints.

4 Footfall

1. See Ingold 2004 and 2011. Also Aldred 2021 and Leary 2014 for more on this from an archaeological perspective.
2. See Amato 2004 for this sort of anthropological study of walking.
3. He mentioned this in an interview in *Vanity Fair*; see Kashner 2013. For the Tuareg, see Gagnol 2021.
4. There is a lot on this, but see Mauss 1973; Farnell & Wood 2011; Lee & Ingold 2006; Ingold & Vergunst 2008. See also Goffman's (1959) classic descriptions of bodily performances in *The Presentation of the Self*.
5. For anthropological literature, see Farnell 1994; 1999; Farnell & Wood 2011.
6. This translation is from O'Sullivan 2011, 32. O'Sullivan 2011 provides much of the inspiration for this section.

7. O'Sullivan 2011 again, but also see Urry 2007 for more on the way people generally express their culture through movement.

8. Translation from O'Sullivan 2011, 28.

9. The point about Roman gait is made by O'Sullivan 2011, 16. For modern gait recognition technology, see, for example, Boulgouris *et al.* 2005.

10. Östenberg *et al.* 2015, and especially Östenberg 2015, and Hellström 2015.

11. Johnson 2002.

12. Jamieson & Lane 2015 for the archaeology of the Pleasance. See also Johnson 2002. Also, Everson 2003 for similar themes at Bodiam Castle in East Sussex.

13. See Gilchrist 1999; Johnson 2002; Jamieson & Lane 2015; Everson 2003.

14. Johnson 2002.

15. See Fairclough 1992. Also, Gilchrist 1999; Johnson 2002; Faulkner 1963.

16. Johnson 2002, 59–60.

17. Fairclough 1992.

18. This section owes much to Beaumont 2015.

19. See, for example, Thomas 2006; Gros 2014; Elborough 2016; Beaumont 2015.

20. See Bradley 1999, and Harding 2003 for similar discussions. See Pollard 1992 for The Sanctuary, and Pollard 1995 for Woodhenge.

21. Kern 2000, 30.

5 Pathfinding

1. See Bell 2020 for more on this.

2. Suggested at least since the nineteenth century – Mortimer 1895. Also see Bell 2020.

3. Darling 2009 for North American song cycles. Chatwin 1987 for songlines.

4. Saunders 2021.

5. See Saunders 2021; Loveday 2016; Brophy 2015 for good discussions of cursus monuments.

6. See Loveday 1998 for a discussion of henges along routeways. Bell 2020 also discusses henges, routes and crossroads.

7. See Vyner 2007 for the 'Great North Route'. See Leary & Field 2012 for more on Marden henge.

6 Pilgrim

1. This whole chapter owes much to Webb 2000.

2. See Gilchrist & Sloane 2005, 84; Gilchrist 2012.

3. See, for example, Simonsen 2019; Webb 2000; Gilchrist 2012.

4. Morrison 2000; Webb 2000.

5. Webb 2000; Simonsen 2019; Labarge 1982.

6. Webb 2000.

7 Overstepping

1. See, for example, Beresford & Hurst 1972.

2. These paragraphs owe much to Beaumont 2015.

3. See Fumerton 2006. The quote from *The Praise, Antiquity, and Commodity of Beggary, Beggars, and Begging*, 1621, is quoted in Fumerton 2006, 56.

4. This and the preceding paragraphs have been informed by Everitt 2000.

5. See Johnson 1996; Williamson 2000.

6. Everitt 2000.
7. See Moxham 2001 for an entertaining account of this.
8. Johnson 1996. See Wittering 2013 for Cambridgeshire.
9. See Debord's 'The Theory of the *Dérive*', 1956, which sets out instructions on how to drift through the city. See also Bonnett 2015 for more recent discussions. For psychogeography, see, for example, papers in Richardson 2015.
10. This has been well written about, but Solnit 2001 provides an excellent summary.

8 Routefinding

1. See, for example, Harrison 2003; or Reynolds & Langlands 2011.
2. Bell 2020; Bell *et al.* 2020.
3. Coles & Coles 1986.
4. Knight *et al.* 2019.
5. See Giles 2020 for an excellent and up-to-date study of bog bodies, and this whole section owes much to that book. See Nielsen *et al.* 2021 for a recent study of the contents of Tollund Man's stomach.

9 Feet follow hooves

1. See, for example, Toulson 2005, 30.
2. See Bozell 1988 for more on this.
3. Larsson 1990.
4. De Waal 2016.
5. See Zeaman 2011 for an entertaining and compassionate description of this relationship.

6. See Liebenberg 1990 for a classic account of tracking.
7. Gooch 2008, 70. This quote inspired the title of the chapter.
8. Toulson 2005.
9. Toulson 2005, 15; also see Williams 2017 for an evocative description of this.
10. Hindle 1998; Toulson 2005, 46.
11. Fox 2012; Toulson 2005; Williams 2017.
12. See Toulson 2005, 8.
13. Noted in Williams 2017.
14. Mitchell 2015, 7 for the 'big dog' reference; Bozell 1988 for the Pawnee.
15. See Librado *et al.* 2021 for the genetic study.
16. See Pollard 2017.
17. The entanglement between animals and humans is a rich source of study in archaeology. For more, see: Brittain & Overton 2013; Honeychurch & Maka-rewicz 2016; Oma 2010; Overton & Hamilakis 2013.

10 Transhumance

1. Fox 2012, 36.
2. Klein 1920.
3. Fox 2012.
4. For an excellent description of booleying, see Costello 2020.
5. See Costello 2018; 2020; Fox 2012; Margetts 2021; Bowden & Herring 2021; Bil 1990.
6. The quote in Ó'Dubhthaigh 1983.
7. This is a subject picked up in Evans 2003.

8. See Costello 2018 and 2020 for an excellent discussion of these places as liminal zones and associated folk stories.
9. Fox 2012.
10. For Wessex, see Sharples 2010 and Fowler 2000; for Dartmoor, see Fleming 1988; for the Thames Valley and southern Britain, see Yates 2001 and 2007; for the Fens, see Evans & Knight 2000 and Pryor 2001; and for northern Britain, see Chadwick 2007, 2013, 2016a, 2016b, and Giles 2012.

11 Wanderland

1. See Bergerbrant 2019 for the Egtved Girl, and Frei *et al.* 2017 for the Skrydstrup Woman. Bickle 2020, and Brown 2014 for Neolithic and Bronze Age movement generally. For Roman female mobility, see Foubert & Breeze 2014; Eckardt 2010; Eckardt *et al.* 2014. For an accessible account on Viking mobility, see Jarman 2021.
2. Brody 2001, 7; and Kelly 1992, 43; 1995.
3. There has been much debate in archaeology about sedentism in the Neolithic, and there is a huge literature. You could see, for example, Whittle 2003, 39–44; 1997; papers in Bailey *et al.* 2005; Cribb 1991 for more on this. Also, Leary & Kador 2016 for a more recent discussion. For large Mesolithic buildings, see Gooder 2007; Waddington 2007; Woodman 1985.
4. See, for example, Kelly 1995; Barnard & Wendrich 2008.

12 Wayfaring

1. See Rackham 1976 and 1986.
2. Kohn 2013; Macnaghten & Urry 2000. See Noble 2017 for an extended discussion of woodlands and archaeology.
3. Noble 2017.
4. See, for example, Davies *et al.* 2003; Coble *et al.* 2003.
5. Solnit 2005.
6. Thoreau 1854, 111.
7. See Ingold 2000 for more on this.
8. Ingold 2011.
9. Ingold 2000 covers these themes and many more.
10. This perambulation comes from the Helmsley Estate and dates to 1642.
11. See Houseman 1998.
12. Johnson 1996.
13. Houseman 1998.
14. As described by Lewis 2000. See, for example, Georgiou *et al.* 2020 for evidence of this in the archaeological record.
15. See, for example, Dickson *et al.* 2003; Püntenera & Moss 2010.
16. See Rudenko 1970.
17. Michael 2000.
18. For medieval pointy shoes, see Dittmar *et al.* 2021; for Dutch clogs, see Vikatou *et al.* 2017.
19. See Michael 2000 for a broader discussion of this beyond archaeology. See Gilchrist 2012 for the quote.

13 Roadrunning

1. See, for example, Brigham 2015.

2. Malim & Hayes 2010 for Sharpstone Hill. Fulford & Timby 2000, 26–8 for Silchester.

3. See Bishop 2014 for more on Roman roads and many of the themes discussed in this section.

4. See Fleming 2009 for the Welsh trod, and Evans 2008 for the trods of the North York Moors. Langlands 2019 for more on early medieval roads.

5. See Hindle 1998; 2016; and Allen & Evans 2016.

6. Prestwich 2016. See also Labarge 1982 and Ohler 1989.

7. See Dunn 2020 for more on corpse roads, including the Shakespeare quote.

8. As noted in Langlands 2019.

9. See Anthony 2007.

10. See the highly entertaining Moran 2009 for more on this.

14 Flowing

1. This example taken from Edgeworth 2014.

2. See Edgeworth 2014 for an archaeological study; and Strohmayer 2011 for a more general, theoretical one.

3. Sauer 2016; Webb 2000; Cook 1998.

4. Edgeworth 2014.

5. See Edgeworth 2011 for an excellent discussion of the archaeology of rivers.

6. Widell 2017.

7. For henges and water, see Richards 1996a & b. For axes in the Thames, see Field 1989.

15 Weatherscape

1. I've written about this previously in Leary 2015.

2. Hulme 2017; Harris 2015.

3. See Harrison 2016a and b; and Mabey 2013 for wonderful discussions of seasons. See Ohler 1989 for a brief discussion of them in the medieval world, and Hosfield 2020 for an extended discussion of seasons in the Palaeolithic period.
4. See Schofield 2009 for an archaeological take on snow.
5. Maraszek 2009.

16 Time's march

1. See Lane Fox 2008 for an interesting discussion of Greek myths and heroic journeys.
2. See Helms 1988 for her classic study.
3. Examples found in Helms 1988, 115 and 126.
4. See Boivin & Owac 2004 for a series of papers on this theme.
5. For jade axe-heads, see Pétrequin *et al.* 2013. For Cumbrian axe-heads, see, for example, Bradley *et al.* 1992 and 2002.
6. Boivin & Owac 2004; Brumm 2004.
7. See, for example, discussions of gift exchange in Mauss 1954, or in an archaeological context, Fowler 2004.
8. Appadurai 1986; Hahn & Weiss 2013.
9. Gilchrist 2013; González-Ruibal 2013. See Olsen 2013 and Olsen *et al.* 2012 for more on an object-based approach.

17 One way

1. See, for example, Will 2017.
2. See Bellwood 2013, and Manco 2013 for good summaries of all the above.

3. See Reich 2018, and Krausse & Trappe 2021 for excellent and accessible discussions of this.

4. Olalde *et al.* 2018; Armit & Reich 2021; Patterson *et al.* 2022.

5. Fitzpatrick 2011 for the definitive account, and from which this description comes.

6. Brace *et al.* 2019; Reich 2018; Krausse & Trappe 2021.

7. See Cohen & Sirkeci 2011 for a discussion of migration beyond archaeology.

8. Will 2017; Shah 2020.

9. Sennett 2011.

18 Seafaring

1. Brennand *et al.* 2003. See Pryor 2002 for an entertaining account of Seahenge.

2. Jarman 2021; Cunliffe 2017; Pye 2014.

3. See Foubert & Breeze 2014 for the Roman postal system; Winchester 2010 for Atlantic crossings.

4. See, for example, Van de Noort 2011.

5. Van de Noort 2011; Cunliffe 2017.

6. See Ferentinos *et al.* 2012 for Crete; and Bird *et al.* 2016 and Norman *et al.* 2018 for Australia.

7. Cunliffe 2017; Van de Noort 2011.

8. Clark 2004. For the analysis of the sand layer, see Green 2004.

INDEX

Index